▶ ADULTS LEARNING
Fourth Edition

▶ ADULTS LEARNING
Fourth Edition

Jenny Rogers

OPEN UNIVERSITY PRESS
Buckingham · Philadelphia

Open University Press
Celtic Court
22 Ballmoor
Buckingham MK18 1XW

email: enquiries@openup.co.uk
world wide web: www.openup.co.uk

and
325 Chestnut Street
Philadelphia, PA 19106, USA

First published 1971. Reprinted 1977
Second edition published 1977. Reprinted 1979, 1984, 1986, 1988
Third edition published 1989. Reprinted 1992, 1993, 1994, 1997, 2000

First published in this fourth edition 2001

ISBN 0 335 20677 8

Library of Congress Cataloging-in-Publication Data
Rogers, Jennifer.
  Adults learning / Jenny Rogers. – 4th ed.
    p.   cm.
  Includes bibliographical references and index.
  ISBN 0-335-20677-8 (pbk.)
    1. Adult education.   I. Title.
  LC5215.R6 2001
  374–dc21   00-050139

Typeset by Graphicraft Limited, Hong Kong
Printed in Great Britain by St Edmundsbury Press Limited,
Bury St Edmunds, Suffolk

▶ Contents

▶ Introduction

When I first wrote this book in 1971, I produced the book that I wished someone had given to me when I was new to teaching adults. Now, for this fourth edition 30 years later, that wish remains the driving force behind updating and substantially rewriting the book yet again. I now know a lot more about teaching and learning than I did in 1971, but the core principles of good practice seem much the same. The context has changed, but the needs of adult learners are recognizably what they were then.

I envisaged the original target reader as someone who was a specialist in a particular subject, but lacked knowledge of how to apply that specialism to working with adult learners. Probably I saw my core reader as working in adult education institutions of one kind or another. Now I see a much broader audience. Many tens of thousands of people are involved in helping other adults learn. There are still, for instance, many lecturers in higher education who have little or no training in how to teach. There are the thousands of management consultants who also train. There are the thousands of consultancies teaching people how to use computers. There are people who are working with adult learners in environments as varied as prisons, cruise ships, leisure centres, medical and nursing schools, community colleges and offices.

The possibilities for learning and teaching seem literally unlimited. The quest for 'self development' means that good old favourites like yoga classes are still going strong, but so too are the thousands of 'be-a-better-person' books. The ultra-rapid pace of change in companies of all sorts as they struggle to stay competitive means that training and development are now open to virtually everyone who is employed and no longer an option or just an indulged pastime of the boy and girlie swots. 'Having a development plan' is no longer the preserve of people who'd been through a hippy stage in earlier life and had never quite got over it, but a sensible strategy for keeping your entire work-force flexible and up to date. Anyone who is a manager needs to accept that they must also be a coach. Leadership is now as much about coaching as it is about setting direction, and coaching is about helping people learn.

The medium through which training is delivered is many times more varied than it was. Where once the only way to learn was assumed to be face to face or with a book, now it can be through open learning manuals, open learning centres, and increasingly by 'e' means, whether through the phone, the Internet or by 'e-coaching'. Whatever the medium or the context, I still believe that the subject is a lot less important than the method. The art of teaching adults is a broad-based and flexible one whose prin-ciples can be applied to a wide variety of situations.

This book cannot offer you any easy, infallible guides to 'good' teaching. Teaching and learning are infinitely variable processes. You and your learners will have particular needs, which only you can interpret. The suggestions I offer are meant to outline a range of possibilities from which you and your group can choose, rather than being a set of rules to which you must always adhere.

It is a hard task to write a book about teaching and learning without sounding prescriptive or saintly – or possibly both. In the first two editions, I did not attempt to explain how and why I had come to write it, perhaps because the experience was still too recent or perhaps because I was sensitive to the possible accusation that I was too young and inexperienced to be writ-ing a book of 'advice' at all. The original book came out of two strands of experience: my own in the classroom and an early career experience with the BBC.

My first job as a young graduate was in a college of further education where teaching adults became an important part of a job which I had originally thought was going to be about the education of 16- to 19-year-olds. To survive and learn your craft in this environment your wits had to be sharp and your sense of humour well to the fore. As the youngest person in my 'adults' class working towards an English exam, I was the teacher but without any of the natural authority that age and experience confer. No wonder that I often felt I was engaged in a role-play rather than the real thing.

In the daytime in the same college, I found myself in some equally tricky situations. For instance, there was a class of 17-year-olds to whom I was 'teaching' economics, a subject I knew literally nothing about. The merciless teasing of my class taught me a great deal about the need to love your subject and the absolute necessity of burning to communicate your pleasure in it.

Where the adult students were polite and reticent, the sparky young people I taught in the daytime never hesitated to give me candid feedback on my performance: 'Bit boring today – too much theory'; or, 'I liked that bit where we read the play instead of you talking'. They had gloriously direct ways of teaching teachers humbling lessons. One day, a group of 18-year-olds was mysteriously late coming into the classroom. Only the two class swots sat there exchanging desultory conversation with me in an empty classroom. After ten minutes of this, I enquired again what on earth they thought had happened to the others. Apparently as baffled as I, they just shook their heads dumbly. Seconds later, the door of the cupboard burst open and out tumbled the other 15 members of the group. 'We know you like discussing things with Tom and Pauline, so we thought we'd play a little trick!' Only 18-year-olds could so ruthlessly and innocently rub home this important lesson. Like many teachers I was talking to the 'good' students far too much. They were telling me that they'd all like a share.

In effect my younger students trained me and I diligently and gratefully applied what I was learning to the adults' classes where the same forces were at work but far more subtly. After all, the adults did not have to be there. If the class was disagreeable, they could simply stop coming. The overriding impact of this experience amounted to one simple message. In teaching, the customer, not the subject, comes first and is always right, and the customer is the learner.

However valuable this experience was, it was considerably sharpened by my next job where I worked as an adviser on adult education to the BBC. If only every tutor could, as I did, sit anonymously in other people's classrooms. The 'mistakes' that we all fudge in our own efforts become burningly obvious when looking at someone else making them. I am reminded now of something I say to the people I train as coaches when alerting them to the dangers of disliking something you see in a client: 'If you spot it, you got it!'

Since no one in adult and further education really believed that the BBC knew anything at all about teaching and learning, I was welcomed everywhere. 'It's only some girl from the BBC' I overheard one principal explain to one of his tutors, 'She just wants to sit in at the back'. So as an honorary invisible woman, I saw adult teaching of all types – probably several hundred classes in all – in the raw. I saw bold and innovative teaching that was years ahead of its time and that would still stand scrutiny today as outstanding. Equally, and perhaps more often, I saw tutors struggling because no one had apparently even attempted to show them solutions to the common problems of all teaching and learning: how to motivate, how to simplify without losing the integrity of the original ideas, how to help people learn.

One piece of good fortune fuelled my desire to pass on to others what I felt I now knew. In my first year at the BBC, I was asked to help evaluate a series called 'Teaching Adults'. The series became a classic and introduced me to some of the best brains in the business. Some of them contributed to the book I edited for the BBC, *Teaching on Equal Terms*, but working on this project made me even keener to write a book of my own, hence *Adults Learning*.

It has been a satisfying book for an author, introducing me to many talented and interesting people and giving me the chance to work as a trainer of other tutors making similar journeys. The original publishers, Penguin, sold the rights to the present publishers, Open University Press. Over the years the book has been translated into several languages including Japanese and Chinese and has sold well in excess of a quarter of a million copies – not bad for something perceived to be an ultra-specialist topic by its first publisher. One of my best moments ever as an author was seeing someone reading it on the underground in London. I am sorry now that I did not follow my instinct and introduce myself to my reader, asking eagerly for feedback. Maybe this was just as well, as the tube is full of crazy people and I don't think I looked very authorial that day.

In the years since writing the third edition, I believe I have become a living case study myself of why adult learning is still such a vital topic. I had had three different careers in earlier life – teacher, internal consultant on education and TV producer. Since then, I have added several more. After working as a commissioning editor for the Open College, I became a manager, running a training department for the BBC. Then, feeling that spending my time on endless 'working parties' (which felt very much like non-working parties) was not for me, I moved again. This time it was to start my own company, Management Futures, where we train, teach, consult and coach. So in addition to continuing training, I have also had to learn how to become an entrepreneur, management consultant, coach and director of a small company.

The 'safe' career is now a fantasy for all of us. This is true for me, for my sons and for my clients. Like so many others, I have needed and wanted to learn new skills as I have shifted into the 'portfolio' economy. I have become computer literate and Internet addicted. I have added satisfying new hobbies to my life, including line dancing, an interest that involves a lot of intensive learning (I am a slow learner here), and which arouses much puzzled amusement among family and friends. I have written several other books, including three on human personality as seen through the lens of psychometric questionnaires. Also, like so many of my contemporaries, I refuse to accept the possibility of the 'R' word. Retirement is not something I can contemplate. I am struck by the truth of one friend's recipe for a happy life: never get divorced, never stop learning, never stop

Chapter 1

▶ Adult learners: what you need to know

Ask yourself what sticks in your mind as the outstanding pieces of learning you accomplished at school or college. My guess is that you are not very likely to nominate sitting spellbound at the feet of a 'great teacher'. It is far more likely that you will immediately remember your part in a particular school play, a project, a trip abroad, an experiment you successfully concluded on your own, the achievement of some sporting feat – all of them active pieces of learning where you were at the centre of the effort. From three years' study of history at university, my mind has wiped most dates, wars, monarchs and all the essays and lectures that went into recording them. If asked, for instance, as I have been by a homework-doing child, why William of Normandy invaded England, and why the industrial revolution started, I could not give a coherent response to either. Yet I can still recall much of the detail of a project in my final year at university when, as a special privilege, we were allowed to research and write up a subject of our choice. The other highlight was joining an archaeological dig at a Romano-British site. I learnt more here in five days about the principles of archaeology than I had in two terms of academic study.

This is the first essential principle of teaching adults successfully and it's a paradox. Teaching is about learning. As the American writers Postman and Weingartner wryly commented: '"Oh I taught them that but they didn't learn it" . . . is on the same level as a salesman's remarking, "I sold it to him, but he didn't buy it" '.[1] You cannot do the learning for someone else. To say 'I learnt him' is not only grammatically wrong, it is also impossible. Therefore your task as a teacher of adults is to become a designer of learning.

In the learner's mind

Anxiety

Let's start with basics. Assume that most of your potential learners are anxious. The anxiety may not last, and if you are doing your job properly, it will soon fade, but some anxiety is probably inevitable. Here are the authentic voices of adult learners talking about how they felt approaching learning:

> For months before this training started I used to dream about looking stupid on it. I was astonished at myself – a Cambridge first and all – being so worried about going 'back to school', but I used to think to myself, oh well, in another three months, two months, one month, it'll all be over.

> I opted to go on a special course for chief executives. The publicity emphasized that it would be very stretching – it was being run by a university business school. I know it was silly, but I felt that there was a severe risk of being out of my depth.

> I enrolled for a basic graphic design course at the local adult education place, but was very nervous about going – in fact I nearly didn't. I'd been working as a web designer already without any formal training and I really thought I was likely to be shown up as a fraud.

> My department is very keen on 'awaydays' but I dread them. It always seems to me that you are put on the spot and have to speak. What if I say something silly?

> I went on a leadership course which was run by people who

had all been actors. It was run in a theatre with the idea that you could learn a lot about leadership by learning from acting techniques. To say I was frightened would be putting it mildly. I have always felt self-conscious anyway and I felt certain that other people would be far more confident and better at everything than I would be.

Memories of school

Why do we feel so negative about learning something new? There are several possible explanations. One is that in spite of all the training and development that now happens inside and out of employment, education is still seen as something that happens to children. To be back in a 'classroom' seems to revive memories of being at school and with it all the associated sub-servient status. As adults we are, after all, people who have acquired the status of maturity in our own and other people's eyes as partners, friends, employers or employees. Perhaps this status and self-esteem is less robust than it appears and is easily threatened when put back in the apparently subservient status of the learner.

This will be more of an issue when people's experience of school education has been disappointing, and even more so where education has involved the ritual humiliation so common in the worst of our secondary schools of all sorts, whether the fascistic rituals of the worst sort of boarding school or the patronizing sneers of the graduate who is forced to teach children he or she despises at a comprehensive school. Don't underestimate the power of these memories:

> My parents thought they were doing a wonderful thing by sending me to a famous boys' school. What I learnt there was the corrupting power of authority. Of course there were some decent teachers there but so many of them were in it for the wrong reasons. Put me in a 'classroom' now, even one in a nice hotel with no sitting in rows or anything like that, and I'm right back there, still aged 13, terrified and

determined to fight back in ways that won't get me into immediate trouble!

Experience of school: constant failure. I was labelled not very bright at an early age because I'd had undiagnosed problems with my hearing. Even now, I see trainers/tutors as hostile to me and expecting me to be dim. I know how silly this is because I realize the kind of people I now encounter leading courses are the absolute opposite, but it takes me a long time to trust them.

When I met my coach for the first time, the thought in my mind was that I was going to be meeting the headmaster. I just couldn't get it out of my mind.

Whenever I go on a residential course, even a really good one, I know I'm going to have the same anxiety dream on the first night – strange bed, don't sleep very well. In my dream, I'm back at school and I'm doing an exam. I haven't revised and I'm going to be shown up. I wake up at the point where I'm faced with an examination paper which I can't answer.

Challenge to beliefs

Another possible explanation is that potential conflict is involved when an adult comes forward for learning. As adults we already have certain well-developed ideas about life along with our own systems and beliefs. To admit that we need to learn something new is to admit that there is something wrong with our present system. Many people, though they may perceive that they do need new skills or knowledge, feel so threatened by the challenge to their previous beliefs that they are unable to learn. I recently ran a short course on leadership for a group of media clients. It was soon apparent that I had a problem with one member of the group – or perhaps to put it another way, he had a problem with me. I put forward some simple and commonly accepted ideas about 'emotional intelligence' (i.e. skill with people) being essential for effective leadership. He loudly challenged me on the grounds that I was suggesting an 'identikit' style of leadership that would 'take all the creativity out of the media'. Of course I was suggesting no such thing. What I was suggesting, however, was clearly a huge threat to his previous assumptions about leadership – and perhaps about his own behaviour, since emotional intelligence was not very apparent in the aggressive way he questioned me!

This may be why adult learners so often take refuge in the idea that what we are learning is really meant for someone else. Many years ago I was part of a group of teachers who had been pressed, perhaps clumsily, to attend a refresher course on basic teaching skills. Even though we all enjoyed ourselves and learnt a lot, it would have been impossible at the time to find a single member of staff willing to admit that the course was aimed at us. No, it was meant for 'very young' or 'part-time' teachers. To have admitted that *we* needed help would have aimed too sharp a blow at our ideas of ourselves as already competent teachers.

I have seen the same thing many times since working as a consultant to organizations. Senior management announces a reorganization. With the reorganization goes a need to acquire new skills, and training is offered as a way of supporting the change. In some organizations, childish resistance to this opportunity can take many forms. My colleagues and I have experienced all of the following: people who write letters or bring their in-trays to the group; people who stalk out dramatically; people who arrive late and leave early . . . the list is endless. The message is clear: we don't like or want this reorganization (fair enough), but also we don't need this learning, we're OK as we are. This will be particularly true where the new learning is also perceived to be a threat to identity. So, for instance, when the National Health Service introduced a much-hated 'internal market' (later unpicked to relief all round) doctors made no bones about their view that they were clinical specialists not business people. As one of my colleagues said at the time, 'If I had £10 for every time I heard the phrase, "this isn't a baked bean factory you know" I'd be a rich man!'

People who work on education programmes in developing countries have learnt the hard way that it is better to face up to the implications of these phenomena than to wait for them to catch you out. If you can run an educational event where the tutor is 'one of us' – literally a member of the community, you probably increase many times over the chances of your message being heard.

Let's not exaggerate this phenomenon and let's accept that it will vary enormously from one person and one situation to another. A young graduate full of confidence with a degree newly in his or her pocket may bounce into a training course with little anxiety. A mature chief executive working on a course with his or her peers may soon lose whatever quivers of worry he or she has experienced beforehand. On the other hand, an adult non-reader may travel over city and county boundaries to make sure of finding a class where he or she will not be recognized. However, my working assumption is that there will be some anxiety wherever there is real learning because real learning involves change, and that's difficult stuff for most of us.

Don't be fooled by the apparent confidence of the learner. One of my clients is a celebrity in his field and widely admired for his ability (known to some for being so clever that he is jokingly assumed to have two brains). He told me much later that he was so frightened at the thought of his first coaching session with me that he nearly cancelled it. And what was he frightened of? 'Ah,' came the reply, 'it was fear of exposure. I felt sure that you would show me up as a fraud.' Since he had never met me, I think we can be sure that this said a lot more about him than it did about me!

Along with your assumption that there will be some apprehension goes a duty to defuse it as soon as possible. There is no case whatsoever for deliberately whipping up anxiety. Anxiety gets in the way of learning – physiologically because it increases the amount of free fatty acid in the bloodstream and makes learning even more difficult. This is why ice-breakers, a bit of early fun and a frank acknowledgement of fear are all a good idea. I say more about this in the section on the first session (see Chapter 5).

Differing expectations

One associated issue may be that your learners have expectations about teaching method and that these are at odds with your own beliefs about the best way to learn. I had a vivid demonstration of this the first time I worked with doctors. This group was on a management development course. There were 24 of them in the room – a big group. My colleague and I had arranged the room 'café table' style – that is, small groups sitting at round tables. This was to maximize participation. Before we had even begun we had heard the grumbles. It was going to be difficult to concentrate; it was going to be impossible to take notes; they wanted to see us, not each other – and so on. And why was this? The answer was clear. Much medical education is still conducted lecture-style where the purpose is giving information to a group which is expected to save its respectful questions until the end. Our assumptions about participation and learning from each other were stoutly resisted. What did they have to learn from each other? We were the experts weren't we? The value of our brief inputs of theory were, in our view, wildly overestimated, and the value of discussion greatly undervalued by the group.

You may see the same phenomena at work where there is a cultural mismatch between tutor and group. A colleague in our firm went to China to run a course. He met with polite bafflement at his attempts to run a participative programme. In the end his group indulged him, but he still feels that they did so only because obedience was owed him by virtue of his status as an expert.

You will not have to leave home to see the same phenomena in some adult education classes. People often want something familiar. Here is one tutor describing this issue and how she coped:

I was teaching French to children during the day using a very good audio-visual method. My adult class nobly agreed to try the same thing. I met my first snag in the first five minutes – no books. No books? They demand books, nicely

of course. I say they cannot have books until they are familiar with certain sounds and patterns. Rebellion subsides.
Second snag, five minutes later. Several of the class sneakily
trying to write things down according to a phonetic script
of their own. I explain about listening and speaking, they
explain they must see things written down. We have this
very polite battle lasting a few sessions. They begin to see
the advantages. I begin to see that they need the reassurance of the written word. Eventually I do give out some
written material and they sigh with relief as at the appearance of old friends. Pronunciation slips a bit, but general
progress seems to be faster.

Now that the case for participation has been so widely and
so well made, you may also see the reverse. I once ran a group
where there was a somewhat doughy theoretical element to be
taught and understood. I explained this at the outset. My group
was disappointed. They wanted 'games'. I explained that games
and the content of our course did not sit neatly together in my
view. If they could come up with a relevant game then I would
be perfectly willing to incorporate it into our event. That was
the last I heard of games, but I was aware that my creativity and
ability to design an interesting programme had been soundly
challenged and that I had failed!

Ageing

Even though we live in a society where the numbers of older
people are increasing rapidly as a proportion of the total popu-
lation, 'grey power' still has a long way to go before it is ac-
knowledged as a real force. This is an ageist society where, for
instance, many companies reject 50-year-olds as 'too old' and
where it is still at the time of writing (2000) not against the
law to state desired age ranges in a job advertisement. You may
find that this prejudice has eaten into the self-esteem of your
learners. However, be assured, and assure them, that research has
demonstrated again and again that when learning is designed

according to robust principles, age differences become less and less important. One classic experiment will make the point. The psychologist Meredith Belbin, later to be celebrated for his work on team roles, was commissioned in the 1960s to retrain train drivers. He and his wife Eunice ran two experiments at the early stages of the work with matched groups of drivers. When offered active methods of learning, age made no difference at all to the drivers' performance.[2]

Assuming there are no physical problems which affect brain functioning, my own experience as a tutor, and now as an older learner myself, is that age makes no difference whatever as long as people are motivated. Motivation is far far more important than any other factor.

Motivation

Why it matters   •

It's so obvious really, but it must be stated. Unless you are motivated you will not and cannot learn. As a tutor you therefore must tap into and keep refreshing the motivation of your group, otherwise the whole thing will collapse.

An animal example will help make the point. We have always kept cats and one of them, Bluebell, was a British shorthair of exceptional good looks but had always been a slow learner and a cat of exasperating blankness. She decided that her litter tray was no longer a suitable place to deposit her faeces and began using a particular place on our expensive carpet instead. Shouting, smacking and speaking sternly have no effect on cats – they simply become more adept at defeating you. Instead I patiently waited until after meals and carried Bluebell gently but firmly to her tray. This did not work. Why was my training a failure? Because Bluebell had no motivation whatsoever to please me. Cats are not pack animals and Bluebell did not care one jot about my good opinion. So I had to think again. What was her motive for using the carpet? Suddenly it occurred to me that the offence occurred most often when her daughter had already visited the tray. Fastidiousness was the problem. Scrupulous removal of this evidence combined with steady supervision produced immediate improvement.

You may feel that this example has no bearing on human motivation, but I believe it does. Bluebell had her own reasons for her irritating lapses. I could not oblige her to learn from my training until I had uncovered what her reasons were. Human beings are hundreds of times more devious and subtle, but the basics of learning are the same for humans and animals. To learn you must be motivated. To teach, you must uncover and sustain the motivation.

Some tutors feel that just being exposed to the subject is enough – people will 'learn by stealth'. Alas, this is not a sensible way to proceed. Can you, for instance, remember the telephone number of the last restaurant you phoned to book a table? Most likely not. You probably learnt quadratic equations for maths GCSE but can you explain them now? Think of the last foreign holiday you took in a place where no English is spoken. What words did you learn there, when you were hearing the language spoken all around you every day? Probably very few unless you were determined to try your hand at communicating in a new language and made a deliberate effort. Unless these are useful pieces of knowledge, being exposed to the information is not enough, we have no reason to learn.

Lack of or wilting motivation is one of the main reasons that learning fails:

I ran a government training scheme. The people on the courses hated them. They saw them as a poor substitute for a job and were resentful about being obliged by threat of losing their benefits to be there. It was a real struggle.

Basically they didn't know why they were doing the course. OK, the organization was introducing a new costing scheme but they were all cynical about whether it would actually happen because so many others had been proposed and then nothing had happened. They didn't see why they had to waste their time – they'd think about it when the new system was a certainty. It was grim. Stony faces, looking at watches and 'when's coffee?'

The upside of this downside is how wonderfully sustaining motivation can be. An adult who is determined to learn something is a fearsome force:

My aim is to pass GCSE English because that is what my son is doing. I have been able to help him a lot and I suddenly realized I might be able to do it myself. I am absolutely determined to do it because I've always thought there was something special about English as a qualification. What has sustained me is the thought of actually getting that certificate. My tutor has been wonderful. She has praised us, nagged us and has kept dangling the thought of THE PASS at the end!

People often ask me what keeps me going as everyone seems to know how hard it is to do Open University work on top of everything else that's going on in your life. It is very hard work but it's simple really. My stepmother and I did not get on very well and she made it clear that I was a financial burden, so university was out. She also implied that I was not bright enough. Although she's been dead for many years now, I know that one of my principal motivators is to prove her wrong on the second count and to feel, on the first, that this is something I deserve and owe to myself. I *will* do it!

Whether adults come to learning willingly or not, the truth is that unlike children, they are free to leave. There may be unpleasant consequences of leaving – for instance, a row with a boss, a failure to get promotion because of lack of a vital new skill or loss of government benefits, but they can leave the training if they wish. They are not prisoners. On the rare occasions when I have a reluctant learner in a group, I always point this out – very kindly and politely – but point it out I do. The presence of a grumbling cynic is destructive to a group and if people are so hostile to learning, and you have done your best to motivate them and they are still obdurate, it is much better for them to go.

Oddly enough, the invitation to leave often takes the steam out of the protester. With another consultant, I was running a high-profile event for one organization where the methodology struck some of the participants as, in the words of one of them, 'manipulative flim flam'. He was expecting high quality theoretical ideas, lecture style, whereas our event was about personal development and the internal barriers to change that we all create through fear. It was indeed a very challenging event, but the challenge created discomfort for him. He threatened to leave and instead of trying to persuade him to stay, I instantly agreed that he should go if he felt unhappy. Looking thoroughly astonished, he said he would think about it. He stayed for the rest of the event.

All reasons are acceptable because any motivation is better than none. All adults will be able to think of attractive alternative ways of spending their time and your event has to compete with those:

> I have a towering in-tray. I'm trying not to think about it while I'm here.

> What do I give up to get here? Watching *EastEnders*!

> At the end of a long day there are great attractions to just sliding off to the pub with the others. It takes discipline to come here instead.

Extrinsic motivators

Adults bring a great range of motivations with them for learning. The simplest to understand are the so-called extrinsic ones – the learning that seems demanded by the learner's situation. Here are some of the most common:

- Promotion may depend on acquiring new skills or on passing an exam. For instance, in the police force, an exam system is an entry-level qualification for promotion – it does not guarantee a job.

- Entry to a new career may depend on acquiring the qualifications that go with it. So, for instance, a secretary wanting to make a career in human resource management will study for his or her IPM (Institute of Personnel Management) qualification.
- More money may be offered to people who have a qualification.
- Change is a powerful motivator. Even people who declared themselves computer phobic now understand that a computer is more than just another kind of typewriter. Information Technology (IT) literacy is fundamental to most jobs.

Intrinsic motivators

'Intrinsic' motivation is harder to grasp because it is not so visible. For example:

- Social motivation is a powerful propellant. Your learners may simply want the pleasure of being with other people. They may feel lonely and isolated. Learning may be their passport to meeting other people.
- Others come to learning because they see it as an important part of a new identity. They may want the yardstick of achievement: am I the kind of person who can learn Mandarin Chinese? Can I satisfy myself that I have the ability to get a black belt in judo? For these learners, the subject is important but so too is the proof they are obtaining that they can do something that they and the outside world think difficult.
- Some motives are straightforwardly to do with remedying some deficiency, real or imagined, which must now be faced.

  I read OK but writing was just a torment. When my son was 6 he began learning writing at school and he just couldn't understand why I wouldn't 'play writing' with him. He pestered me so much that I couldn't bear the shame of it any more. A local scheme found me a tutor and it was much easier than I'd thought. The worst bit was admitting to someone outside the family that I couldn't write.

This story and the many others like it was behind the modest success of the Adult Literacy Campaign of the 1960s and 1970s. Interestingly, the campaign found it much easier to recruit tutors than students, a difficulty which remains today. Any survey of functional literacy estimates anything between 20 per cent and 25 per cent of adults to be poor readers and writers.

The pleasure of learning

Whatever analysis you make of the motivation of your learners, you will find that there are always some in any group who are simply there for the pleasure of learning:

> I have always loved learning. It gives me the kick other people might obtain from cocaine or booze. I have bought many part works and I own a set of encyclopaedias. I've joined many courses in and out of work. In my organization the head of the training department says I'm her favourite course junkie!

While it's important for you to know what the motivation is of your learners, remember that initial motivation is just that: the bundle of hopes and fears that people bring to the beginning of a piece of learning. It can be changed. In a successful group it grows and develops. In an unsuccessful group it shrivels and dies: this is a defeat for the tutor.

Maybe the truth is simpler. Learning is a natural part of being alive. As long as you are alive you can go on learning. To learn and master a skill, a piece of knowledge, to acquire a new outlook on a problem is a normal and fundamentally satisfying human process. For myself I am as proud of now being able to swim 1000 metres elegantly as I am to have passed an Open University examination. I am currently very pleased with myself today as I write for having at last mastered one particularly difficult dance and to be considered one of the more advanced students in my dance class. All these achievements have cost me time and effort. My true motivation is opaque to me, but does it really matter? I was ready for learning. I often find the process frustrating. I have been humbled by my inability to get past the blocks of my own mediocre performances, but I persisted. Now I take pleasure in knowing that all that effort was worthwhile. Surely this is what it is all about. Learning is part of a circuit that is one of life's most fundamental pleasures. Your role as a tutor is to keep the current flowing.

The essence of learning

> It has in fact been established that if we were to reverse the natural order of things and keep children away from school while sending their parents there instead, we could teach the parents the same thing for about a quarter of the expenditure in time and money.
>
> (John McLeish)

> I hear and I forget
> I see and I remember
> I do and I understand.
>
> (Chinese proverb)

Let's assume that your students are highly motivated. You understand that they might be feeling anxious and you have techniques ready to allay their fears. But this still leaves other questions. How do you guide learners through the substance of your subject? What are the best ways to engage their interest? Is it actually harder for adults to learn quickly than for children? Are there any special methods that should be encouraged or avoided with adults?

There are some simple rules of thumb based on research, experience and common sense which can help give answers to all these issues. First, remember again that it is important to distinguish between teaching and learning. You can be teaching away vigorously but your students are not necessarily learning:

> I have never in my life had such terrible teaching as on the course I did on industrial law. I swear the lecturer would never have noticed if the whole class had played noughts and crosses because once he'd started it would have taken an earthquake to stop him. His method was to introduce

the topic, say 'Any questions?' and then before anyone could answer, plod on in a deadpan way non-stop for an hour and a half. The content was so dense that it was impossible to remember. He gave out some notes but these weren't much help because they seemed to cover different ground.

Here was a tutor who had prepared conscientiously, who probably left his classroom drained by the effort of talking for an hour and a half, but whose students had learnt nothing.

The importance of short-term memory

This is one of the few ways in which children and adults differ. As we grow older, our short-term memory capacity becomes less efficient and more easily disturbed. What seems to happen is that our brains receive information and scan it for meaning in order to decode it at some time in the future. If this scanning stage is interrupted, the information never passes from short-term to long-term memory.

In everyday living we experience this as a minor nuisance: for instance, forgetting an eight-digit telephone number as soon as we have looked it up. Where learning is concerned, any method that relies too heavily on short-term memory is doomed to failure. This means that lecturing and demonstrating on their own are poor methods to use with adults. The reason is that the words of the lecturer or demonstrator are perceived by our brains as a never-ending series of information slabs. Each successive slab interferes with the storage of its predecessor. The result is the phenomenon we all know; the feeling that we have been fed a mass of information, all of it undigested.

This has important implications for all teachers of adults. It means that if you rely on any verbally-conveyed method of giving information, you are unlikely to be helping your learners learn. You may enjoy it, your group may even enjoy it if you are a good performer, but they will probably not be learning. The core art of teaching adults is to find alternative ways of conveying ideas and information.

The learning cycle

This idea was first mooted by the US academic, David Kolb, and has been given further life by the two British writers Peter Honey and Alan Mumford. Their *Manual of Learning Styles* spells out the practical implications for learners and tutors.

Essentially, the concept is that for learning to be successful, you need to go through a cycle of learning:

- activity – doing something;
- reflection – thinking about the experience;
- theory – seeing where it fits in with theoretical ideas;
- pragmatism – applying the learning to actual problems.

So, for instance, let's suppose you want to learn how to design a garden. In the *activity* phase, you might, with a tutor's help, have a go at actually designing a small garden with a particular aspect and set of problems – let's say it is a small town garden with dry sandy soil, facing east and shaded by large sycamores from a neighbour's garden. This would involve you in making a number of decisions about materials, costs and planting. Having done that, it would be useful to *reflect* on it, standing back, getting feedback perhaps and observing how other learners have solved the same problems. You might then consider the *theory*: what rules of thumb there are for using particular materials or for dry, east-facing, shady gardens? At the *pragmatic* phase you might return to the original plan, revising your ideas in the light of everything else you now know.

The importance of the learning cycle is more than theoretical. We all have natural preferences for different styles. These may be slight preferences or be very pronounced. Some people may be equally at home with all four styles, but mostly adults will have developed greater comfort with one over the other three. This will affect you as a tutor because your natural tendency will be to emphasize the styles *you* are comfortable with. It will also affect your group because they will have their own preferences and areas of comfort. So, for instance, if you as a tutor enjoy the activist style, you will want to run events which have a high degree of *doing*. You will build in a lot of variety – perhaps getting people working in small groups for much of the time with a lot of discussion. There will inevitably be people in your group whose preferences are for the reflective style. They may well find the relentless pace imposed by an activist tutor to be overwhelming because it gives them no time for their favourite style which is to think, stand back and reflect.

There can be strong likes and dislikes associated with each of the styles. Table 1.1 gives some brief descriptions.

Table 1.1 Likes and dislikes of different learners

Style	Like	Dislike
Activists	Doing and experiencing. Enjoy games, practical activities, anything that's energetic and involving.	Sitting around for too long; working alone; theorizing; having to listen to others droning on.
Reflectors	Time to think, observe, take it all in first; love to watch others; need some solitude and above all, time.	Being hurtled into activity, having no time to think; crammed timetables; lack of privacy, no time to prepare.
Theorists	To know where something fits in to overall ideas and concepts; analysis and logic; being stretched; abstract concepts; structure and clarity.	Frivolity, mindless fun; wasting time; not being able to question and be sceptical; lack of a timetable and proper structure.
Pragmatists	Practical problem solving; relevance to 'the real world'; learning that answers the question 'How can I apply this?'	Anything airy-fairy and theoretical; learning that makes too many references to the past or the future and avoids drawing attention to NOW.

Implications of the learning styles

The first challenge is to know yourself. Which of these styles are you naturally drawn to? Whatever your answer, remember that many of your learners will have different preferences. When designing learning, remember to touch on all four styles as far as possible, not just your own favourite.

Remember, too, that different subjects and circumstances will have their own imperative. For instance, if you are teaching people how to drive a car, there is probably no great place for theory – to drive a car successfully does not depend on knowing how the internal combustion engine works, though to pass the driving test you do need to know the Highway Code, a reflective activity. But mostly, learning to drive needs an activist approach. It cannot be learnt through reading books. If your subject is management development, you may be drawn by the attraction of the many US gurus and their books – a theoretical approach. However, your learners may only want the pragmatic answers: What can I apply from this to my own work and job? What really works?

Varying the pace

Imposing one pace on a group is not an effective way for them to learn. Perhaps you vividly remember, as I do, the yawning boredom of schooldays where the main method of learning was hour after hour of being talked *at* by the teachers. At my school, as the 'top 5 per cent' we were initially 'creamed off' from our age group, and were then ruthlessly streamed again. Even so, there were wide differences of ability according to subject and aptitude. At gymnastics I was slow and cautious. I struggled in the middle bands in science subjects. In arts subjects I was often bored by waiting for others to catch up. If the pace is fixed to suit the fastest it will demotivate the majority. If it is right for the middle band it will alienate both the brighter and the slower learners.

The more you can design learning so that people can work at their own pace, the more effective it is likely to be. This is not because competition is ideologically unsound, but because it doesn't work. With adults this is especially important. The older you are, the more likely you are to want to sacrifice speed for accuracy and the more likely you are to want information before making a response.

Scores of different experiments have shown that if adults are asked to learn something new under time pressure, the older they are the more likely they are to become confused and to make mistakes. Where no clock-watching is involved there is no difference in performance.

When no allowance is made for the increase in individual differences which age and experience bring, when decline in short-term memory is ignored and when tutors simply plunge on bearing the whole load of information-giving themselves, packing every moment with fresh and complex detail, then some situations of monstrous futility can develop:

> I came to nursing as a mature entrant and I nearly left it for the same reason. I could not bear the monotony of sitting for hour after hour where you were treated like children and where the facts came at you in a steady stream. No attempt was made to involve us in the learning: the only thing that mattered was passing the exams. It was like a convent school full of silly adults!

In manufacturing industries set-length training periods have been abandoned as wasteful because they impose one pace on all. It is always better for adults to measure their progress against their own previous performance rather than to attempt frantic rivalry with their neighbours. People start with different kinds of knowledge and work at different speeds.

Relevance

While of course it is true that there are people who are drawn to learning for learning's sake, most adult learners are strongly motivated by wishing to acquire skills and knowledge they can use in practical ways. The nearer you can make the learning to the 'real' world, the more acceptable it will be and therefore the more quickly and effectively your students will learn. The obverse is true too. Offer adults learning that they consider irrelevant and they may well resist:

> To help me get through my accountancy exams, my firm paid for me to go to classes at a finance training specialist. I regarded it as a necessary evil. The content of the exams was so far removed from the way we actually did the job that the poor tutors had to follow the same silly 'rules'. They were constantly apologizing for it, saying that they knew we didn't need to know this or that thing, but it was on the syllabus and could appear in the exam papers. It had virtually no relevance to my job and I resented every minute I spent there.

Your skill as a tutor is to make the training resemble the real task, even if some of the distractions and complications of reality have to be stripped away:

> I wasn't sure how far you could 'learn' negotiating, but I went along. It was excellent because all the exercises were based on exactly the sort of situations we meet every day. We started with simple two-handers and then went on to more elaborate scenarios using the same principles and finished with team exercises. Some people felt it was artificial because you didn't have all the information that you would have for real, but I felt that was actually a help. It allowed me to see the basic principles pretty clearly.

The importance of relevance holds good for any situation where adults are learning, even when the students are people whose intellectual capacities are well below the norm. One tutor of adults with learning difficulties reported their indignation at having to practise handling money by using cardboard coins. She was forgiven this blunder only when the rightly despised cardboard was replaced by the real thing.

In the past, much vocational training ignored this need for realism and relevance. This led to the establishment of the National Council for Vocation Qualifications (NCVQ), a body which endorses the idea that only the skills needed for the job are the ones that should count as a qualification. NCVQ has had mixed success. It has been more successful at entry level than for senior level qualifications. However, the principle is sound, as is the movement to accredit prior learning. If you can demonstrate that you have competence, then you should get the qualification. And competence means you can produce the same excellent performance under the eagle eye of a trained observer every time.

Traditional knowledge, and lecturing as a way of providing it, still has a grip on some professions, notably medicine. Some years ago I was involved in writing a manual on cardiopulmonary resuscitation as part of a campaign in which I was involved. Traditionally, all first-aid manuals begin their instruction on resuscitation with a description of how the lungs work. There is usually a drawing of the heart and lungs and a description of the exchange of oxygen. I felt that knowing how the lungs worked was not necessary in order to revive an apparently 'dead' person and that the usual drawing of red and blue pipes and sponges was a distraction from learning the life-saving routine. Distinguished doctors on our advisory group stoutly resisted this departure from tradition over many hours of argument. If I had not been vigorously supported by some influential younger doctors, I doubt that I could have had my way. That manual eventually won a Plain English Award, but I notice that the current edition of the joint Red Cross/St John *First Aid Manual* still has the same old drawings!

Reinforcement and practice

Without reinforcement, skill and knowledge will fade quickly. The basic principles are easy enough:

1 Find out what existing knowledge your learners have. Let's assume for the sake of argument that in subject X your learners know nothing.
2 Analyse whatever you are teaching into its component parts.
3 Start with the pieces of learning that fulfil these criteria: they are basic building blocks; they are easy to learn.

4 Reinforce them through practice until people have thoroughly 'internalized' them – that is, they can do them accurately without conscious thought.
5 Slowly add more building blocks, making the learning more complex.
6 Reinforce through more practice.

Sounds easy doesn't it? In reality you will need immense subtlety to apply these principles. What is *enough* where reinforcement is concerned? How do you know whether you are going too fast or too slowly? What happens when you have a group which contains very mixed abilities? Is it possible to break down a skill so far that it loses its resemblance to the real thing?

The dance classes I attend as a learner are an excellent example. Such is my love of dancing that I go to classes wherever and whenever I can, and since I travel a lot I have sampled classes in many different places. I have probably been taught now by perhaps 30 different teachers. All are teaching the same dances (they come and go in popularity just as pop music does) to similar groups of people. I see huge variations in effectiveness. Some can barely be bothered to teach the steps, hurrying through the demonstration of a new dance, pleasing the minority in the group who are talented natural dancers but dismaying almost everyone else. You can spot these teachers by the large numbers of people who sit out any dance that is in any way complicated. At the other extreme are the patient plodders who break down every dance into tiny, slow sequences, going through it many times without music, re-teaching every dance every week on the assumption that no one in the group will have remembered the steps. These teachers also lose people because the pace is too slow for many of their students. One such teacher in particular breaks each sequence into such tiny, slow fragments that it loses its resemblance to the dance and becomes unrecognizable. The effect of this intended helpfulness is, paradoxically, to make the dance much harder to learn.

Only you and your group can judge what the answers are to such dilemmas. One of my own rules is never to compromise the integrity of the subject by oversimplifying. So, for instance, if I am teaching influencing skills, I do split the various techniques into identifiable parts which can be practised separately, but I emphasize that real situations involve using any or all of the techniques together.

If in doubt, ask the group. Look for feedback from how people are responding. In a dance class it is easy to see, even if the teachers sometimes don't spot it. People just don't do the dance very well if they haven't had sufficient reinforcement and practice before trying the dance with the music. They will need to do it again if they are going to remember it properly. There will be similar tell-tale signs that you will spot with experience in your own groups.

If you have dropouts from a continuing course, follow up the non-attenders and ask what their reasons are for not coming (don't assume that this is anything to do with the course; it may not be). Ask for feedback specifically on how much practice and reinforcement people need. If you are overdoing it, step up the pace. If you are underdoing it, add more.

Catch them doing something right

It is important to design this phase of learning carefully for one simple reason. As adults, once we have made a mistake, it is much harder to unlearn it than it is for a child. It is as if once that trace has been made in the adult brain, it is difficult to replace. This is particularly the case with any 'kinaesthetic' skill – dance is again a good example. If I have literally put a foot wrong in learning a new dance, I find my foot making the same mistake over and over again, in spite of my brain telling my feet what to do.

As a tutor, your challenge is to design activities that give your adult students a high chance of getting it right first time. Wrong first time will more often than not mean wrong for some considerable time afterwards. This leads to discouraged, demotivated learners. Where you see a mistake, correct it straight away. The sooner you do this, the easier it will be for the learner to do better.

Using adult experience

The best-designed adult learning aims to minimize the disadvantages and maximize the advantages of the experience adults bring with them to learning. It can still be the case that trainers and tutors of adults bemoan the fact that their students are not the nice blank sheets presented by children. One of my clients, for instance, tried to instruct me to recruit only people under 30 as trainees for his new team on the grounds that people under 30 would not have had time to learn bad habits.

As adults we have had experience of the world and probably also some experience of the subject we have decided to learn. For this reason we will usually have a great deal to contribute, even if we are also much more likely to be sceptical and to challenge the 'rules':

> My most enjoyable groups have always been with women students who want to take up teaching after rearing their families. They simply will not accept pat theories and glib statements about child development because all the time they are asking, 'Did my children do that?', or, 'Was that true when my children were four?' Whereas a 20-year-old will write it straight down in her notebook, the mature woman always pauses to weigh and consider against her own and other people's experience. She always sees the ifs and buts. In these groups, by relating the students' experience to the general view, I feel we finally create a tremendously lively and complex picture of child psychology. They bring a depth and humour to rather dry theories which younger people could never attain.

This university teacher found her experience of teaching mature students rewarding precisely because she relished their wish to challenge. The same phenomenon can be unsettling if you are unused to it:

> I was working on a regeneration project which involved working with groups of people who had been unemployed for a long time. My role was to help them acquire job-search

skills. I found out the hard way that you couldn't just give them rules. They constantly challenged me on the grounds that I didn't know what it was like, I'd never been unemployed and in their experience interviewers didn't behave the way I was suggesting. I knew that they needed my help but I wasn't getting anywhere. The penny dropped when I sat in with a colleague and saw how she handled it. I saw how she didn't make statements or lay down the law. She opened up the topic, asked for opinions and experiences and drew the advice out of that. It's much harder to do this than I'd thought and it took me several months to learn to do it as well as she did.

It is essential then to solicit and use the experience of your learners. Failing to do so risks rejection of your message. More positively, by inviting comment you eventually arrive at a much richer and denser picture of the world and one that is therefore more relevant to real life. The more learners are involved and offer their own experience, the more they are likely to learn at speed.

This involvement is also important for another reason. Suppose you encounter the downside of adult experience: the stubbornly entrenched view, the commitment to one particular technique even if it is incorrect, the hidden gap in knowledge. Meredith Belbin again contributes some salutary lessons from his early work. When asking a group of trainees how many sixteenths they thought were in an inch, several said 'ten' and others thought there might be twelve. How are you to counter such mistaken assumptions if you don't know what they are? How are such students ever to learn if they are never obliged to hold their experience to the light so that they can see the holes in it for themselves?

Arousal

As adult learners we are more experienced and world-weary and we often need a good jolt to the system before we can start learning. This can be particularly true of groups meeting in the evenings, but applies more generally too. Most of us will be preoccupied, often still half thinking about other responsibilities, and in the evenings simply tired. For this reason an intensely involving first few minutes is always a good idea at the beginning of each major session, especially perhaps any session that begins straight after lunch when my own private view is that human beings were designed to have a nap.

You will devise your own activities as appropriate to your subject, but here are some ideas from other tutors:

Five minutes of warm up exercises – gets people stretching and changes the mood as well as being fun.

I play a silly game called 'Bat and Moth' which involves people standing in a group and chasing each other. It has no purpose other than to get people moving!

I start my maths classes with five minutes of mental arithmetic – fast and fun.

Everyone has a piece of paper and I ask them to write down what their distractions are. I then go round the room with a box and ask people to crumple up the paper and put it in the box. It's a way of acknowledging that we all have distractions and we can physically set them to one side.

I ask people to describe what percentage of their attention I have. Answers vary from 20 per cent to 95 per cent. I then ask what needs to happen to get to at least 95 per cent. It's fun and I get a lot of useful information too!

Such techniques are successful because they have certain elements in common:

- everyone in the group takes part;
- to do them at all you must be involved;
- they are fun.

Learning to learn

Can adults learn to learn? All the evidence suggests that the answer is yes. First, experience of learning improves performance. People who have kept mentally in trim by maintaining a consistent diet of learning tend to do better than otherwise identical learners who have not. The reasons seem partly to do with practice and partly to do with confidence.

You can speed this process where appropriate with some simple, well-designed activities intended to help people improve their learning techniques. Depending on the course and the subject, you can achieve sensational improvements by showing people how to do note-taking, memorizing, rapid reading, essay writing, answering multiple-choice questions, and so on. If you are running a group where there is formal learning of any kind, it is often useful to build such help in the early weeks of the course.

Putting the learners at the centre

The most effective learning happens when we can fulfil these criteria:

- we really want and need the knowledge;
- we know how we will apply it;
- we will be rewarded one way or another for having it;
- we can draw on our own experience;
- we can learn at our own pace and style;
- we are stretched and challenged;
- we are supported;
- we are treated as an individual with unique needs by whoever is helping us learn.

Apply this list to any serious learning you have done in your life. For instance, if you are a parent, this is probably the most challenging role any human being can ever take on. How did you learn the role? Think about professional learning: where and how did you acquire your most useful skills? The answers are likely to be that in both these cases you learnt them on the job. The challenge for a tutor or developer is to accelerate this natural process a hundredfold by using the basic principles of learning described above. When you do, it is surprising how freeing it can be. For instance, both *action learning* and *self-managed learning* have taken these principles to their logical conclusions.

In *action learning* a small group of learners meets regularly for a day or half-day. There might, for instance, be six people, all senior managers in the same sector but from different organizations. Each member in turn puts a live issue in front of the others. The role of the group is to work through skilled questioning, challenge and support – not advice. The aim is for the problem-holder to gain new insight into their issue through having five or six other minds working on it. In turn, this problem-holder then becomes a listener for other people's issues. Although the learning is generalized, the focus is pin-sharp on what is relevant and useful. Group members learn how to listen without judging, they learn how to support and challenge without getting either too involved or too threatening.

In *self-managed learning*, the same principles are at work. For instance, there are now several postgraduate degrees along the style pioneered by Ian Cunningham at Roffey Park in Sussex. These are run on the principle that there is no set curriculum. The courses whip away the security of being 'just' a student with all the dependency (and counter-dependency) this can produce. As a learner, you and only you are responsible for your learning. The framework can be startlingly simple:

- What do I know I know?
- What do I know I don't know?
- What don't I know that I don't know?

The course begins with the task of producing a learning contract. Each learner's contract will be different, but it will answer questions such as:

- What's my experience in this field?
- Where am I now?
- What do excellent people in this field do?
- If I want to be excellent in this field, what do I need to know?
- What literature is there in this field that I need to read?
- How will I get to my goals?

- How will I know I've got there?
- What evidence will I produce for the rest of the group and its tutors to prove that I have?

This first phase ends when every learner's contract has been assessed by every other learner – note, not just by the tutors. If it is too easy or too hard, it must be adjusted.

The second phase of the work will typically be about carrying out a project which will meet the criteria each learner has agreed. The final phase is assessment. Again, this will be done by the whole group, not just by the tutors.

This approach to adult learning is too radical for some. It will not work where there is any element of *licensing* necessary – for instance, any profession where chartering is essential. Its critics worry about 'soft options'; they yearn for the safety of the curriculum and teacher-in-charge power of the traditional learner–teacher relationship. However, these approaches put the learner firmly at the centre, managing their own learning. This surely has to be the aim of anyone who is serious about real adult learning, whether as student or tutor.

Chapter 2

▶ Giving feedback

The old saying that practice makes perfect is not true. But it is true to say that it is practice the results of which are known which makes perfect.

(F.C. Bartlett[1])

Giving 'feedback' and criticism, praising and commenting, these are all so important in learning that the topic deserves a whole chapter to itself. Teaching adults is complicated enormously by the difficulty of 'criticizing' an equal. Not giving the right quantity or quality of feedback is one of the main reasons why adult learning fails, so it is worth thinking about how to get it right. Basically, there are two dangers: giving it in the wrong way and not giving enough:

I went to a two-day workshop on how to give presentations. I was one of only two women so I felt conspicuous anyway. It was run by a management training consultant, but 'in-house'. I gave my first little presentation and I knew it was bad – I was so nervous I could hardly speak. The trainer's comments were devastating. I was utterly destroyed. I'm afraid I broke down and cried. The next day I just could not bring myself to go into work so I missed the second day. The whole thing was so mortifying it makes me cringe now to think of it. I learnt nothing; my terror of speaking in public was worse than it had ever been and my credibility with my bosses took a long time to recover.

My first experience of learning as an adult was a complete damp squib. I'd enrolled for a jewellery class at a very good

London Institute. The tutor was a well-known craftsman but had no experience of teaching. He was a good demonstrator, but nothing more. I slaved over my little projects, but I never got a *crumb* of comment from him. He'd look at my efforts and would just say 'Hmmmm . . . yes' and pass on. What did this 'Hmmm . . . yes' mean? 'Awful'? 'OK'? 'Boring?' 'Beneath contempt'? I never found out! I went on going to the class because the facilities were wonderful and the other students very friendly. We helped each other, but it would have been so much better to have had comment from him.

Feedback matters, because without it the learner is unlikely to improve. Imagine that you are one member of a group whose task is to throw a ball over your shoulders at a target. Your group does not receive any guidance on whether the balls are hitting the target. There is another group which does receive guidance. Who is most likely to hit the target most often? Your group is going to continue haphazardly making the same errors over and over again. The other group will steadily improve. This simple and classic experiment has actually been performed and the results showed over and over again that, without feedback, performance cannot improve.

If performance does not improve, then all learners, but particularly adults, quickly lose interest: their motivation flags, and without motivation there can be no learning. Adults are rarely obliged to continue with a learning project against their will. By the time we have reached adulthood most of us are adept at slithering away from situations where we feel we perform badly.

Good feedback is one of the basic rewards of learning and is therefore a critical part of the learning cycle, shown in Figure 2.1. If as a tutor you break this cycle by failing to give the right kind of feedback then the learning will fail – as happened in the 'presentation workshop' quoted earlier. What is especially sad about this example is that the learner blamed herself, whereas in fact the failure was the tutor's.

To put it more positively, the sensational effect of just a little well-judged feedback can surprise even an experienced tutor:

Figure 2.1 The learning cycle

Although I was an OU tutor for many years, it never failed to amaze me what effect my comments had. It was quite common for students to ring me after they'd had their TMAs (tutor-marked assignments) back and to say things like 'You've no idea how many times I've read what you said'; 'I felt *thrilled* that you'd given me that mark'; 'I was thinking of giving up, but you've encouraged me so much I'm going to carry on'. Often I'd only written about 15 lines, but it was enough to make all the difference to a student who'd been wondering whether to give up or not.

When to give feedback

There is a simple rule about the optimum time to give feedback on learning: *give it as soon as possible.* Don't wait until either the triumph or the error is repeated. Give it immediately. The reason is that learning is like quick-drying paint. You only have a short time to correct the mistake or let it harden into a permanent error. If something is wrong, then put it right straight away. If all is well, then say so and say why and the learner can speed on to the next stage. If there is a mistake, help the learner put it right on the spot. The best time to give comment is while the effort of making the attempt is still fresh and the 'arousal' effect is still there. Leave it until later and learners may have settled back into complacency, or into an environment – home, for instance – where your influence is more easily resisted:

I was sent on a 'safe-handling' course as my job involved lifting. I thought I'd done OK, but I heard on the grapevine that the tutor thought I was being 'bolshie' and that he'd tried to correct my technique in various ways but I still couldn't quite get it. I was furious. For a start he'd told us that the course was confidential and there'd be no feedback to our bosses. But also, if there was a problem, why didn't he say so? I didn't remember him trying to correct my technique at all – he hardly seemed to register that I was there. I felt very let down and I still don't know what I'm doing wrong – if anything.

How to give feedback

Here we come to the heart of the skill of teaching adults. As a tutor you are the peer of your students. Indeed many of your students may, in their non-student roles, be the kind of people who may rightly make you feel humble. You cannot rely on being their 'superior' in age, income, social class or occupation, only in your knowledge of your subject. Because of this, it is your right and your duty to comment on their efforts. The problem is how to do it effectively while leaving them with their dignity intact.

It is often said that 'we learn by our mistakes'. I have often thought how thoroughly misleading this statement is. It would seem truer to say that we learn by our successes, *as long as we know why we are being successful*. First, we have to accept that as human beings our craving for praise and reassurance is utterly limitless. Praise makes us feel secure and confident, where negative criticism makes us insecure and self-doubting. But we can only learn from praise when we know what we are being praised for. Let's return to the example of the ball thrown over the shoulder at a target. Suppose you achieve a bull's eye and your 'tutor' says only 'Yes, you hit the centre'. Would you know for sure what it was in your performance which achieved the result? I should say that this was unlikely. By contrast, your tutor might say 'Yes, good! You hit the bull. The reason was that you flicked your wrist to the right just as your hand reached shoulder level'. This feedback is much more likely to help you repeat your success, for three reasons:

- it is given promptly;
- it contains the encouraging word 'good' – your tutor sounds pleased at your achievement;
- it gives detailed comment on *how* you achieved an accurate result.

Giving learners reasons for their success or failure is thus one absolutely fundamental rule for helpful feedback. Don't just say 'That was a good piece of work', or 'Well done'. Always give the reason: 'That was excellent because it was so neat', or 'Good – you looked confident, your nerves were under control and your voice was at just the right level'. However, for feedback to stick and to be even more effective, this process has to be two-way:

I see a number of people who are not formally trained 'tutors' doing brilliant jobs. There's one chap who is superb: he is a good craftsman himself, but his trainees produce beautiful work in what seems like a very short time. When I watched him I realized that this is because all the comment on their work is a *dialogue*. First he sets the standard by showing them what perfect bricklaying or carpentry looks like, and he even produces some 'shoddy' examples for comparison. Then he takes each trainee's effort and discusses it with them so that they are spotting for themselves what the problems and good points are, and how they happened, and then they are pointed to finding a way for themselves of putting it right.

This mixture of gentleness and ruthlessness can be difficult to achieve. It is pointless to put all the onus on the hapless student by demanding brusquely, 'Now what was wrong with that?' Many students will babble on guiltily in such circumstances without any real idea of the justice of their self-accusations. It is far better to establish a constructive dialogue which helps students compare their own performance with the ideal and which helps them diagnose strengths and weakness for themselves.

This puts responsibility where it belongs: on the learner, not the teacher.

It is usually best, too, to concentrate on only a few aspects of performance, whether good or bad. There is a limit to what most of us can absorb at a time without either intellectual overload or (if we are being criticized) damaged self-esteem:

> I was a tutor on a literacy scheme. I discovered early on that marking every single error in the writing was totally counterproductive: the students just couldn't take it, it was too dispiriting. Instead, I concentrated on about three significant mistakes each time. The improvement was usually staggering.

As well as concentrating on just a few mistakes at a time, try to make your feedback unambiguous and clear. In an effort to avoid being 'hurtful' some tutors wrap up their comments in so many layers of qualification or anecdote that the main point is obscured. It is better to say straightforwardly what the problem is, to give the reason, and to leave it there. For instance, suppose you are training a new young manager in how to write a memo. Your trainee produces a reasonable effort, but it is too long. Your feedback is best delivered as some warm words of praise for whatever has been done well, and then a few succinct sentences saying that the draft is too long and why. You should avoid garlanding your comments with anecdotes about your own first efforts to write memos, funny memos you have seen in the past, or office gossip about the addressee. Enjoyable though this may be, especially for you, it will obscure the impact of your feedback.

There is one other common temptation which you should resist. If you see a mistake, don't march in, pick up the work and 'put it right' by doing a large amount of it yourself. As the expert, you know how to do it; it is the students who have to learn by doing it themselves.

Some teachers who rightly pride themselves on the standard of their own work, sometimes find their students' mistakes too painful to contemplate, and will often seize the work and do the difficult bits themselves, sometimes under the impression that students are grateful for such professional additions. There may be occasional students too placid to object, but most people feel cheated if someone else does all the hard work for them. They want the satisfaction and sense of achievement of learning to cope for themselves. They may find the tutor's well-meant interventions hard to endure, as in this art class run by a teacher whom the student earlier described tactfully as having 'tremendous enthusiasm but lacking method':

> General instruction is given *ad hoc* . . . moreover, in dealing with someone's problem, his enthusiasm leads him to paint half the picture himself, instead of merely demonstrating and suggesting and thereby letting the student feel that the picture was 'all their own work'. This makes everyone cross, but no one has had the courage to tell him we don't like it.

It is also better to leave the learner to work out the solution: you can suggest that the memo might be too long, but the details of how to achieve a better length should be up to the learner. Prescriptive feedback only postpones the problem to another occasion because it is your solution not the learner's.

There are various other kinds of unhelpful feedback. One is the sort that is so generalized or vague that it leaves the learner completely stumped: 'You should try to be a bit more assertive . . .', or 'Your work lacks dynamism . . .', or 'It would be better if there were more light and shade in your performance'. All these are vague, waffly statements capable of dozens of different interpretations and quite unlikely to result in improved performance. Then there is the feedback that appears completely subjective: 'I don't like the way you paint clouds', or 'I prefer a different kind of analysis myself'. Learners will be much more likely to reject such comments as personal prejudice than if they are rephrased more objectively: 'There are lots of other ways to paint clouds . . . one of them is . . .'.

Another trap is to offer feedback on aspects of performance that people are simply unlikely to be able to improve because of circumstance or fundamental personality: for instance criticizing a woman javelin thrower for not having the same powerful arm action as a man, or telling someone that their accent is difficult to understand. Whatever feedback you offer, it should always be possible for the learner to act on it.

One principle is fundamental to the whole idea of constructive feedback: criticize the performance, not the person. All good tutors convey their liking and respect for their students and their longing for them to improve. This is the quality in good teachers that is most essential for success, hardest to pinpoint and impossible to counterfeit, but we all know it when we see it:

> He just burnt with a wish for us to know what he knew . . . we *knew* we were the best class he'd ever taken and yet all his classes felt like that . . . We all knew that we individually were the students he cared about . . . and yet we knew he had no favourites!

> It was an extremely supportive atmosphere: very caring, very friendly, yet she was utterly ruthless with us. Sloppy effort was not allowed, the words 'I can't' were banned. Whatever criticisms were made, they were made knowing that she really urged you towards improvement and achievement because she liked you and had faith in you.

There is one simple test of 'pure' feedback. It should offer fact and description, not opinion. This applies equally whether you are praising or pointing out a mistake. If you say 'that was brilliant', or 'that was awful' you are offering an opinion, not feedback. As soon as you offer facts without interpretation, you are giving feedback. Here are some examples.

A learner has completed a role-play where she has to ask a boss for a pay rise. You are running the role-play. Genuine feedback is a comment along these lines: 'When you got halfway through, I noticed that you looked away from me and then began to wring your hands a bit. The effect it had was to make me feel as if you weren't going to push me for the rise'. It would not be genuine feedback to say 'You looked lacking in confidence'.

I have found it useful over the years to distinguish feedback from criticism. This is not just a semantic difference. There is a great deal of difference in both technique and impact on others. At a big yoga class, I overheard the following comment from the teacher to one of his students: 'You totally lack suppleness – you are hopeless!' That student left at the break having, I hope, told her teacher why. A different kind of comment, genuine feedback, will have a different impact. For instance, saying 'You are locking your elbows and knees. That's making it difficult for your body to be as supple as it could be'.

Being on the receiving end of criticism is devastating. Over the years I have collected comment on what it has felt like. It's always the same, regardless of people's experience or seniority:

- Made me feel like a 2-year-old.
- I felt really frightened – wondered what she was going to say next.
- Felt humiliated, hoped others couldn't hear the comments.
- I wanted revenge – immediately – for the loss of face. How dared he?!

Table 2.1 lists the differences between feedback and criticism. As a tutor all your comments should be the sort in the left-hand column.

I once had the opportunity to compare two tutors teaching rather similar courses at the BBC, and to see these different

Table 2.1 Differences between feedback and criticism

Feedback	*Criticism*
Designed to improve performance positively	A way of unloading anger and disappointment
Calm	Angry, tart, dismissive, emotional
Tough on the performance	Tough on the person
Specific – describes the facts	Vague, generalized, uses words like 'you always' or 'you never'
Focuses on the future; makes suggestions about positive alternatives	Looks backwards
Two-way – solicits the learner's opinions	One-way

styles in action. The first tutor, whom I shall call 'John' had on paper a textbook-correct course. The objectives were clear, the curriculum looked interesting and perfectly paced. 'Andrew's' course looked, and was, hectic, competitive and over-full. Yet students ended John's course rebellious, unhappy and disappointed by the small amount achieved. There were even rumours of fisticuffs. Andrew's students, by contrast, gave him an end-of-course champagne party and forgave him the torment he had caused us by piling on work and stress. Why was this? The answer seems clear. John's course, for all its apparent perfection, was marred by his biting, sarcastic comments on our work, by his inability to remember our names or departments from one session to the next and by his refusal ever to offer praise. Andrew's comments on the other hand, though often severe, were never hurtful. He would recall our improvement from previous exercises, showed he never forgot our backgrounds, would offer praise for achievement, looked us in the eye, smiled, nodded encouragement and cheered our little successes. Even now, many years later, I still think of him warmly and feel grateful for the rigorous technical standards I acquired, thanks to him.

One aspect of Andrew's technique holds good for any tutor: always offer some praise and offer it before the negative comments. However poor the performance, there must be some aspect which is praiseworthy:

> Our pottery teacher was wonderful. He used to call us together two or three times in the course of the class and say 'Look everyone, we all *must* see so-and-so's pot – it's so terrific – see the subtle glaze (or the slip, or the way the handle was put on). Isn't it *wonderful*! Just a teeny problem with the shape here – that's because of problems with X or Y – but *very* exciting!' I thought this was very clever. So-and-so glowed at the attention, learnt from mistakes, high standards were established, and a terrifically companionable atmosphere emerged. Somehow, by lucky chance, everyone's work achieved this spotlight over the course of the term!

Where a group combines commitment to high standards with a friendly, non-competitive atmosphere, another benefit emerges: students will begin to offer constructive and useful feedback to each other because they are following the example set by the tutor. It may even be possible to arrange exercises where they specifically do so by working in pairs and offering feedback to each other.

Although 'public' feedback can be useful with a secure and friendly group, in general it is safer, certainly at first, to give feedback privately. Comments on essays should be written for that learner's eyes only; thoughts on how to improve a skill are best delivered one-to-one and without eavesdroppers.

A vital part of any feedback session is agreeing what needs to be done to build on success and correct any mistakes. This should be entirely a two-way process. Make any suggestions you have, then ask the learner what he or she suggests. Your own suggestions may strike the learner as too demanding and difficult, or sometimes not demanding enough. This could be an ultra-brief process or protracted, depending on the circumstances. As a learner in my large and busy dance class, I would be astonished and pleased to have more than a few seconds of my teacher's time. When I was qualifying to administer psychometric tests I expected (and got) 20-minutes worth of comment and discussion when I fell into a difficulty.

Another way of achieving the same end would be to arrange a brief meeting to agree a couple of action points which would include further practice in areas of weakness.

The point of techniques like this is to make sure that the feedback has been heard, understood, and will be acted on in the future. It is easy to forget that what you think is crystal clear may not always be understood by the learner:

I went to a residential weekend on photography. The setting was beautiful, the food excellent, the other students fun, but I didn't learn much. It was most frustrating. The tutor was eager to give me comments on my efforts, but he was in another sphere with 'f/this' and 'aperture-that' – it was all just a muddle in my mind. He would end by saying

'OK? Is that clear?' I'd just nod – I couldn't bear to say that it wasn't clear at all – I'd have felt even more of a fool. Then at the next session of course he'd look exasperated because I'd made the same mistake again and would say 'But I explained all this to you before!'

So giving feedback demands skill as well as tact. The secret of making sure that the message has been 'heard' is to ask open-ended questions like 'Now, just to make sure you've understood, you explain it all back to me', or 'Would you like to summarize what you think we've agreed?' or 'How are you planning to put all this into effect?'

Avoid closed questions which invite the answer 'yes' or 'no' – for instance 'Have you understood?' or 'Is that all right?' Closed questions do nothing to test whether the learner has really absorbed the feedback you have given. Look instead for questions beginning 'Tell me', 'How' or 'Why'.

Finally, be generous with the overall amount of feedback you offer. Most teachers, in common with most managers, grossly overestimate the quantity of feedback they give. I once worked with a man who was notorious for reducing trainees (men and women) to tears of rage, frustration and humiliation. One of the reasons was his refusal (or inability perhaps) to give them feedback other than the occasional highly critical comment on their work. When tackled about this he looked at me in genuinely blank innocence. 'Surely they know', he said, 'that if I don't say anything, I must approve . . . and that even if I do have a criticism, I'm giving them nine out of ten?' Alas, the opposite was true. The few comments he did make were assumed to represent dozens of silent criticisms held back only by intense restraint and dislike of 'scenes'. Some of the young trainees he actually held in highest esteem were the very people who believed he thought little of their work.

To avoid misunderstandings of this sort, the guiding principle is that in every teaching session you should find ways to offer every learner some feedback. This may simply be through a self-checklist in a book, a how-did-you-do conversation with a partner, a private or public brief discussion on performance, written comments on an essay, an action plan for further training or a semi-formal session on general progress.

In giving feedback to learners your own skill as a tutor is severely tested. The possibilities for misunderstanding are endless, the risk of being hurtful or seeming personal ever-present, the temptation to say nothing, or to say too much, ever-looming. But without feedback, your learners cannot learn and as a tutor you cannot be said to be 'teaching'.

Chapter **3**

▶ Understanding your group

> Your students often don't realize that you are as nervous as they are – perhaps that's just as well!
>
> (OU Summer School tutor)

> My company does 'open access' workshops on key management skills. These workshops are very expensive for the learners or their companies; the group usually consists of ten nervous or sceptical individuals: they *know* what it's costing in fees let alone in opportunity costs to their companies while they are away from base. This puts me under considerable pressure to *deliver*. The result is that even after several years of experience, plus knowing that what we do is excellent and well-proven, I never start a new course without 'nerves'.
>
> (Management consultant)

> One's dread is that someone in the group will be more 'expert' than oneself! Or that they might refuse to try some of the projects . . . or that there will be subtle undermining of one's leadership . . . it's all possible. Fortunately, it rarely happens, but the mere thought is enough to give some quivers of apprehension before one starts.
>
> (Training consultant, petroleum industry)

This chapter is about tutors and their groups: how do learning groups behave? What teaching styles work best?

Anxieties

As the quotes at the beginning of this chapter show, worries about learning are not confined to learners. All teachers worth their salt feel some apprehension before beginning a new course. Will you know enough about your subject? Will your material last for the appropriate time? Will the participants like you? Will the teaching you have planned be at the right level for the group? What if some of them drop out?

Schoolteachers who also teach adults often find this a particularly pressing problem. In school a teacher may feel no uncertainty about how to behave with the children. Schoolteachers are always older than their pupils, have the advantage of a longer education and can lean heavily on an established authority structure and tradition which is familiar to everyone. Even a sixth-form teacher faced with an unusually bright and mature set of pupils can take some comfort in longer and 'superior' experience. Not so teachers of adults. They may be younger than all their students, and may even be less intelligent; there is no familiar system or tradition to work in; they may be totally isolated from colleagues. They may have had no training whatever in teaching; the only distinguishing mark between themselves and their students may be their particular expertise in their subjects.

The tutor's influence

It is absolutely correct to have some worries about a new course group, but both the problem and the solution are in your own hands. Your influence is the most important single element in setting the style of a group; as great or even a greater influence on the whole occasion than the sum of all the other individuals. This will come as no surprise to experienced tutors, who will have noticed with dismay how even with a group of apparently stable and self-possessed adults who contribute a good deal to an active discussion, their own moods of exhilaration, pleasure, boredom or irritation are invariably conveyed to a class, and that these reflections from their own personality are in some degree returned as mirror images in the way participants behave to them and to each other.

Your leadership style

Time and time again, research work has shown how critical the style of leadership is to the success or failure of any venture, including learning.

In one of the most often quoted field studies of a type initiated by Kurt Lewin and his followers in the 1930s, the behaviour of three different types of leader was observed. A group of 10-year-old boys in youth clubs were in turn placed under three different types of leadership: 'authoritarian', where the leader was stern, bossy, encouraged competitiveness, punished those who misbehaved and made all the important decisions; 'laissez-faire', where they did virtually nothing – for instance, remained withdrawn from the boys unless directly asked a question; and 'democratic', where the children themselves decided what they would do, and regarded the leader as someone who could effect individual solutions of problems. All three leaders set the groups various handicraft tasks. In the authoritarian groups the boys were submissive and well behaved on the surface while the leader was present, but showed signs even then of submerged aggression, often 'mishearing' instructions or 'accidentally' damaging materials. Among themselves they were competitive and mutually disparaging. When the leader left the room they tended to abandon work instantly and to run about noisily. The laissez-faire groups did almost no work whether or not the leader was present. Under democratic leadership the boys worked well together without fear of one outdoing the other. There was little tension or aggression in the atmosphere, and, unlike the boys from the authoritarian group, some of whom broke up their models at the end of the course, all the work was regarded as 'ours' and treasured accordingly. The temporary absence of the leader made no difference to the amount of work the boys did.

This study remains a classic of its kind, especially as it shows that the same boys behaved differently with each leader. Subsequent laboratory experiments and field studies with adults have repeatedly shown that a friendly, understanding leader or tutor who encourages members to take an active part in events, including taking responsibility for procedural decisions (like when to have a break, or whether or not to smoke), will greatly improve the effectiveness of the group, producing greater spontaneity and more initiative from individual members. Dominant, aloof, authoritarian tutors tend to produce either very hostile or very subdued group members. Where actual learning is measured, the authoritarian-style group may produce more if what is being learnt is straightforward, with only one type of 'right' answer encouraged. On the other hand, where a change of attitude is involved, the 'participating' group is clearly superior.

There is some evidence, too, that creativity is more strongly encouraged in groups where the tutor does not dominate, and a good deal of evidence that the participatory group is the one most people prefer, perhaps because this is the type of group where pleasant social relationships are most likely to develop. The more people talk to one another, the more inclined they are to like one another. It is clearly much easier to retain an irrational dislike for someone you hardly ever talk to than for someone with whom you discuss and argue. Don't make the common mistake of forgetting how important these relationships are to learners because you are so preoccupied with the learners' relationship with *you*.

Working in groups

Some work has also been done on the effects of deliberate competition both between different groups and between individuals. For instance, in one experiment a class of students was divided into two to discuss problems; one group was told that individual contributions made in the group would count towards their course marks, the other group was told that it was the group score which would count. In the competitive group the students were not really interested in what other people said, not friendly to one another, and produced stereotyped answers. In the cooperative group the students enjoyed themselves more, produced a greater variety of solutions, and were relaxed and friendly towards each other.

There has also been a good deal of general research into how small groups solve problems, with the idea of finding out whether it is truer to say that many hands make light work than that too many cooks spoil the broth. Common sense suggests that this will depend on what the problem is, and that it will also depend on what range of intelligence or experience is available in the group, as well as on who decides whether one solution is 'better' than another. Research here has tended to confirm that on tasks such as crossword puzzles or mathematics, which demand concentrated individual attention with only one right answer, individual solutions may be reached more quickly than group ones. But on problems, say, of politics, human relations, philosophy or the performing arts, or any subject where there might be any number of solutions, a group of people produces a far more varied and stimulating range of ideas than an individual.

Remember, too, that the cooperative group can become a powerful way of encouraging individuals to feats they could never manage on their own. Alcoholics Anonymous is one well-known example, WeightWatchers is another. In both these organizations people who by themselves have failed over a number of years to cure addictions have achieved astonishing successes with the help of a group. In teaching terms, many students who have struggled on their own with a subject can find new strength from a group, even if the skill they are learning is essentially – like solo singing, for instance – an individual activity. Perhaps it is just as Thomas à Kempis said, that 'it is the solace of the wretched to have companions in their misery', or perhaps the group really does have a dynamic effect on individual capabilities.

Summing up the differences between the extremes of tutor style, there are considerable implications for the daily business of how you conduct the course. In the student-centred group members will have discussed the aims of the course and will have themselves decided what methods are to be adopted. In the group there will be a constant exchange of ideas among participants and a high degree of individual activity and co-operation on the part of each participant, whether in discussion or creative craft tasks. Such a group will contain members at many different levels of skill and intelligence who can work together satisfactorily. The tutor's role in this sort of group will be to protect and encourage individual members, to develop a high degree of sensitivity and expertise in interpreting the feelings of the group, and to be seen by them primarily as a leader rather than as a subject expert. In many ways the tutor becomes just another member of the group. The main criterion of success in such a group is that participants will feel able by the end of the course to go on learning on their own, having become capable of planning and extending their own learning.

In the tutor-centred group, on the other hand, the tutor will decide the aims of the course and will expect the participants to conform to them. Those who cannot conform will tend to drop out or be made to feel uncomfortable if they stay. The tutor will do most of the talking, and if there is any discussion it will tend to be initiated by or directed at the tutor, rather than take place between participants. The tutor will tend to see participants as a remote mass rather than individuals, and will dismiss the idea that they might be hurt or discouraged by his or her comments, or lack of them. Such tutors will emphasize their remoteness from the group by sitting apart from them and by refusing or finding it difficult to mix with participants on equal terms, or to admit to ignorance or to having made a mistake. They will encourage competition among participants. There will be frequent use of tests and examinations to grade and assess participants, resulting in a group where the people are streamed by ability, and where only the able survive because the tutor finds it impossible to cope with different standards of ability in the group. Participants will become completely passive and dependent on the tutor as the source of all information and are unlikely to develop much on their own.

The solution is to think of the possible range of teaching styles as a continuum which runs from 'tells the group' at one end through 'sells to the group' somewhere in the middle, to 'consults with the group' at the other end. There could be times during a course when any one of these styles is appropriate. Skilled tutors aim for a 'best fit' between these elements:

- the task;
- the time available;
- the group and its needs;
- you, the tutor, and your needs.

If, for instance, time is running out and you have to give instructions about equipment needed for the next session, then you are unlikely to have time to consult the group about their own preferences on equipment. You simply tell them what to do. On the other hand, if you are trying to change behaviours, then neither telling nor selling is likely to be effective. Learners have to make both the 'problem' and the 'solution' their own:

> I run giving-up-smoking classes at the surgery. These people are usually heavily addicted smokers who *mostly*, but not quite, want to give up. I have found over the years that it is quite pointless telling them they *must* stop, even with all my 'authority' as their doctor. They've all heard the health messages many times. The commitment to stopping has to come from them. I run the group by drawing from them individually and as a group *why* they want to stop, best ways of stopping, how to cope with lapses, etc. etc. This way I achieve roughly an 80 per cent success rate. 'Telling' was no good – they dismissed me as a goody-goody spoilsport!

For all that, you may occasionally have to use a 'telling' style of teaching, there seems little doubt that participation and 'consulting' is a better general model. When learners contribute, they are involved and involvement of a challenging kind is one of the main routes to learning.

The group life cycle

> It was chaotic at the beginning. Rival factions from different departments, standing up making speeches denouncing the others . . . people sulking, threatening to leave – awful!

> I could have stood on my head at the beginning in that group for all the reaction I'd have got. I felt like coming in

with a false moustache or a clown's nose to see if it would even have surprised them. Personally, I participated like mad, they never did.

How can you get a good discussion going with 40 large adults who sit in a room designed for 20 small children? No wonder the sessions seemed to be a bit stodgy.

Handling groups of learners can be tricky. A group has its own life and behaves in its own way and this is different from the way the individuals inside it will behave. Being prepared for some of the problems is essential if you are to be its leader.

There are several useful theories which can help you understand that how groups behave can form a number of recognizable patterns. A classic of this sort was described in a well-known paper in the 1970s.[1] Tuckman and Jensen described a typical cycle of group life.

At the *forming* stage, the group is still uncertain. People are polite – there is a false consensus, a pretence that everything is all right. Members are wary of one another. Conversation remains at the level of what one of my colleagues calls 'ritual sniffing': 'What's your name?'; 'What's your job?'; 'Where are you from?'; 'Did you have to travel far to get here?' In a learning group, people will look to you to provide a sense of safety. Politeness and a sense of distance will be the prevailing feeling. There are no cliques but also there is no sense of belonging. People are still figuring out whether or not they want to be in or out of the group.

As the group's business progresses, it will reach the *storming* stage. The pseudo consensus has broken down as people begin to realize that they don't all share the same assumptions and beliefs. People become bolder. Conflicts emerge, either between individuals in the group or between the group and its leader/tutor. At this stage the preoccupation – of group and tutor – can be 'Who's really in charge here?' You can expect challenges to your leadership, even if they are reticent ones of 'Excuse me, but I've done this before' or 'I'm finding this harder than I thought'.

It is a mistake to ignore the conflicts that develop at this stage. If you do, sure as anything they will rise up to haunt you later. Sometimes there will be direct onslaughts on your authority and you need to deal openly and confidently with these, too:

> I was teaching the techniques of job-searching to a group of long-term unemployed adults. This was tricky anyway because we are an area of very high unemployment. On the second day, the whole thing nearly collapsed. Mutterings about 'it's all very well for him – he's got a job' turned into openly hostile verbal attacks by one half of the group, while the other half sprang to my defence – 'give him a chance – anything's worth a try'. I calmed the whole thing down with great difficulty and suggested that we started again. The ones who were angry were given a lot of time to say what it was about me that had caused such attacks and the rest were given their say, too. I retrieved it by the skin of my teeth – but it was a crisis, no doubt about that.

At the *norming* stage the group has settled down. A pecking order has been established, people know each other better, they have accepted the rules and probably developed little subgroups and friendship pairs. In a short course – say, of a day's duration – all these stages can be passed through with great rapidity:

> First session – quiet and cautious. Second session – glances of irritation exchanged at 'things people say'. Coffee break. Third session – the break in the clouds . . . they've talked during coffee and have discovered that other people are not so awful after all. Fourth session – purposeful: emergence of jokes, sense of where people are going. End of day – people are exchanging addresses and phone numbers!

So at the final stage, *performing*, the group glides into action. Now they exist as a group with their own roles and rules. If you let them, they may well always sit in the same seats; they will enjoy group tasks and will carry group loyalty to great lengths. At this stage, the group has a life of its own; its power to support learning is very considerable:

I went to a two-day assertiveness course organized by my company. It was very well run, but the best thing about it was the amazing feeling that developed very quickly in the group. The other women were so terrific – for instance, if someone who had been really shy managed a more assertive role-play, there would be spontaneous applause. People spoke warmly to each other about their efforts. I've rarely seen anything so inspiring ... it made us all achieve feats that would have been impossible alone.

A group does not reach the 'performing' stage by accident. It is the natural and positive way for groups to develop, but it happens because that is the way the tutor has nudged and pushed it. This sort of triumphant conclusion to a course is usually the result of a great deal of conscious effort and skill on the part of the tutor:

Best of all we had an end-of-session party to which we all contributed food and drink. Very enjoyable it was too! This was an unofficial meeting in our own time, but just before the end Mr R., who had spent most of the year making ribald jokes at my expense, presented me with an elaborately wrapped parcel containing an enormous box of chocolates and, on top, a beautifully written 'poem' dedicated to the group and listing in doggerel verse the various idiosyncrasies of the members – including one lady's habit of doing her revision in the lavatory! They insisted upon my declaiming this to them. It made a very suitable epilogue – with just the right touch of ironic banter – to what had been a very entertaining and I think mutually rewarding group.

A final stage is often added to this framework to include *mourning*. This is the stage where the group faces the prospect of its own disappearance. Where a learning event has been powerfully gripping and emotionally stretching, we often feel huge reluctance to leave. The group has become safe, nurturing, a place where 'real life' has been successfully kept at bay, where maybe new discoveries have been made in the company of others making the same journey. It can feel horrible to contemplate the ending of the group. This is why so many people swap addresses, often knowing in their heart of hearts that they will not, as promised, keep in touch. It is always unlikely in the extreme that the group will ever reassemble exactly as it is at the final moments of a course, even where individuals do form lasting friendships.

What can you, as tutor, do about this? When your group has run well, the answer is probably nothing. The responsibility is for the whole group, not just for you. However, there are some simple ideas you may like to consider to ease the pain of separating.

- Offer a follow-up day where people can get together again to review their learning.
- Have a closing ceremony of some kind. These are like ice-breakers in reverse. Little ceremonies that I like and have seen work well include:

Getting people to stand up and form a circle. You then throw a soft object of some kind from person to person. The task is to say one sentence about the programme, which sums it up. A colleague of mine uses a small fluffy pink cat with a silly smile on one side of its 'face'. As it lands, it lets out a maniacal laugh. She calls it 'Giggles'. You continue until everyone has had a turn.

On long programmes, have a gift ceremony. Everyone puts their names into a hat and each name is then picked out. You then buy a tiny present for the person whose name you have pulled out (strict cash limits apply) and give it to that person saying something about what they have contributed to the programme.

Have a bottle of champagne and a glass for each person. Put these into the centre of the room and sit people in a circle. In turn, each person gets up, pours themselves a tiny amount of champagne, and says something which is a toast to the group. Amazingly, even in a group of 20, there is always enough for everyone and the last person gets the largest amount of champagne.

Ask everyone in turn to identify in one sentence the most striking thing they have learnt and one thing they will now do differently.

Sit people in a circle and put a 'talking stick' on the floor in the middle (could be anything – a real stick, a flipchart pen, an object which has some symbolism for the group). Ask people to come forward one at a time, take the stick and say something about the meaning the event has had for them.

Have a party. It is not chance that tutors running residential programmes speak of the last day of the programme as Hangover Day.

Relationships within the group

As well as patterns which can explain whole-group dynamics, you also need to think about relationships between individuals, including those between yourself and group members. Again, there are some useful theoretical ideas which can explain phenomena which would otherwise seem troubling.

Replaying family roles

This is subtle stuff. Growing up in family groups gives all of us imprinted experience of what it is like to be part of a group. We learn roles there that we can be tempted to reproduce at any point when we are once again in groups. So our experiences of being children (less powerful) and how we coped with parents and teachers (more powerful) create patterns that can become permanent. So, for instance, if you were the petted youngest in a large family, you may easily fall into the role of indulged baby in a group. If you were the responsible first-born, you may find yourself always being the person who puts their hand up for extra responsibilities in a group. If you were the family clown and were rewarded for that with laughter (i.e. this was a strategy that got you attention) then you may still be the person who relieves tense moments with a joke. If you were a middle child who found that it was enjoyable to lead a subversive us-against-them revolt, children against parents, then you may be tempted to do the same in an adult group. As a tutor, your own attitudes to power and dependency will have been formed by experiences like this. Your own will be unique, of course, but ask yourself what connections there are for you between your feelings of confidence, or lack of it as a tutor, and your experience of growing up. I would be surprised if there were none.

Similarly, each member of your group will have their own patterns. These will appear in any learning group, though neither you nor they may know their origins. Where you see persistent patterns of behaviour in group members it is worth considering whether this kind of dynamic may be at work.

Transactional analysis

This is a thought-provoking set of ideas, originated by the psycho-analyst Eric Berne. He wrote a best-selling book called *Games People Play* which stormed to popular success in the 1970s. It became so successful that many of the concepts of transactional analysis (TA) have passed the stage of being psychoanalytical and have become clichés. So phrases like *games-playing*, and *win-win* are now widely understood, even by people who have never heard of TA.

TA has much to offer tutors and trainers. This is a postage-stamp sized explanation of what it is. Berne suggested that at any one time we are all in one of three 'ego states'. He called these 'Parent', 'Adult' and 'Child'.

Parent state judges and tells. How we do this will depend on our own experience of being parented. Parent state has two variants, controlling parent and nurturing parent. Controlling parent is bossy and uses words like should, must and mustn't. Nurturing parent suggests, soothes and takes care of others. Both in their way are interested in control and responsibility. *Adult state* is unemotional and factual. It is detached, rational and logical and is the state we are in when we are problem solving.

Child state also has two variants, Natural Child and Adapted Child. When we are in Natural Child state we are playful, creative and can enjoy life. Adapted Child is resentful, rebellious and insecure.

There is no assumption in TA that Adult state is the best state to be in.

The transactional part of TA is where it become most interesting to tutors. Any conversation is a transaction. Remember we are always in one state or another. So if you and your group are in logical problem-solving mode, everyone may be in matching Adult states, and that could be fine. However, if you are in Controlling Parent mode, you may, in TA language, 'hook' the Adapted Child in your group, producing resentful or subversive behaviour. A striking example of this was recounted to me by a colleague:

> I was running a course for senior people in a particular sector. They were an exceptionally boisterous group and got very drunk over dinner one night, making a lot of noise. We had the hotel almost all to ourselves, but there was one elderly couple also eating in the dining room. I felt so embarrassed I felt I had to go and apologize to them for the noise. They were very gracious but I could see they were a bit put off by the racket. The next day I still felt very angry about what I saw as bad behaviour and before we started the morning's session I told them what I had done and also that I had been ashamed to be part of the group. There were a few minutes of silence, and then they really laid into me. Told me that I couldn't take responsibility for them, they weren't children, they were offended, how dared I. They reduced me to tears. I carried on, but with the greatest difficulty.

In this example, the tutor had gone into Controlling Parent State and had hooked the Adapted Child of several members of the group. As they became angrier and angrier with her, they also went into Controlling Parent and she went into Adapted Child. She described this incident as one of the most upsetting in a long career in this kind of work. It certainly illustrates how

Controlling Parent is not often an appropriate state for a tutor. Nurturing Parent may be more so, particularly at the beginning of an event when the need to feel safe may be the predominant one in your group. It is worth thinking, too, about the value of Natural Child State. Groups often need to play and be creative – i.e. be in Natural Child State – and so do tutors. Staying in any one state the majority of the time is likely to be a limitation. For instance, if you rely too much on adult state, you will probably strike your group as overly cool and detached. If you are in Nurturing Parent State too much you could come across as a Mother Hen, refusing to allow the chicks to grow.

Another useful concept from TA is the *I'm OK, You're OK* framework. I like to think of this in a slightly different way, as two axes. One runs from 'I value me' to 'I don't value me'. The other runs from 'I value you' to 'I don't value you'. When you put them together, they form a matrix with four options (see Figure 3.1).

Where you are on this matrix will probably depend on your early experience. For instance, if you grew up with loving parents who cherished you and encouraged you to cherish others, then you will value yourself and others – the ideal place to be, resulting in a confident, sensitive human being. If you grew up constantly criticized and told you were a failure and other people were cleverer, nicer and altogether better than you, then you will value others but not yourself. This will probably result

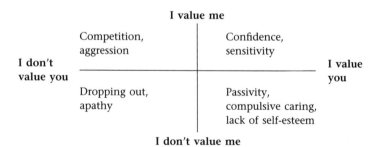

Figure 3.1 The value matrix

in lack of self-esteem and constantly seeking to please others, keeping danger at bay through compulsive caring or avoiding responsibility. If you grew up believing that you were a person of no importance and that others could not be trusted either, then you will be in the 'I don't value me' and 'I don't value you' area – a place where feeling powerless and out of control leads to abdicating all responsibility for yourself and others. The final position is where you value yourself but don't value others. This is often the result of a childhood where there was at least one dominating parent. The child eventually gives the dominating parent a taste of his or her own medicine and learns to discount the feelings of others through relentless competitiveness and aggression. Each of these can become life positions.

Some questions to ask yourself about TA would be:

- Which state are you typically in when you are running a group?
- Do you use all the states?
- Do you over-use some at the expense of others?
- Which transactions are typical for you? What are their typical consequences?
- Which of the life positions is typical for you? How does this affect your attitude to power in a learning group?
- How do you typically deal with participants who are at any position on the matrix other than 'I value me, I value you'?

Difficulties

Let's suppose that you are committed in principle to a participatory style in teaching. It is still possible for things to go wrong. Here are some of the common difficulties.

Talking too much

I was once myself a member of a class in seventeenth-century drama which was taken by a tutor who frequently told us that he was committed to full participation by students in the process of learning, that our learning was to be a mutually cooperative venture, and that he expected to learn as much himself from the class as we did. In fact, although a person of considerable wit and charm, he also had such an autocratic and impetuous temperament that he talked most of the time himself, answered at least half his own questions because he could not tolerate the potential embarrassment of a silence, and occasionally conducted what were indeed vigorous and searching discussions, but always with the same three or four most naturally voluble and perhaps most able students. He made a few token efforts to coax speech out of the others, but gave the impression that he probably never noticed how little they responded. By the end of a ten-week course the numbers had reduced to below half the original large enrolment, and even among the survivors there were two people who did not utter a single word in 20 hours of class contact.

One classic piece of research in the 1950s confirmed how little teachers may know objectively of their own part in lessons. Alvin Zander made a study of four teachers of adults who claimed to be committed to student participation, and found that on average they lectured for 27 per cent of the time, matched each student's contribution with one of their own, and made nine out of ten of all the procedural decisions.[2] Other research has tended to show how teachers may have no idea how much attention they are paying to particular students. In one study of a class of 26, the teacher was found to be giving more than a quarter of his attention to the well-adjusted pupils who presumably did not need it. Even after he had realized this, he found it extremely difficult to distribute his attention more fairly.[3] Many teachers will recognize it as a familiar temptation to go on encouraging those who need little encouragement, and to avoid the difficult and perhaps painful or embarrassing job of helping those who may be silent, moody or unstable.

There is a simple solution to talking too much: stop. The difficulty is that the tutors who are prone to doing it are usually totally unaware that there is a problem. There is a rough and ready test for finding out if this could be your problem. Ask yourself two questions:

- Do you always follow a comment from a learner with one of your own?
- Are there people in your group who rarely if ever speak?

If the answer to both these questions is 'yes', then it will be worth taking stock of the situation – perhaps by asking a trusted colleague to observe you and your group in action.

Showing off

Here is a more subtle variant of talking too much, a hangover from the university tradition of great Oxbridge teachers who draw hundreds of students to their lectures. The number of people capable of carrying off such a feat is actually remarkably small: in the 1950s and 1960s there was the English literature guru, F.R. Leavis; in our own time there is the philosopher and mathematician, Stephen Hawking, and there is only a handful of others.

None the less, the tradition spilled over into adult education in the earlier years of the twentieth century at a time when the working class was thought to be in need of rescue through Workers' Educational Association and university extra-mural education. The tradition still survives today, particularly in parts of adult education and training where students can be apparently quite happy to sit back and let the teacher get on with it. Richard Hoggart, himself an outstanding teacher of adults, has some wry words of warning which stress both the attractiveness and the dangers of this trap:

> The urge towards a generalized charismatic relationship, that way of showing off one's own personality which ends in the rhetoric of a lay preacher, is the strongest of all temptations. You have to learn to suspect those evenings when you feel a throb come into your voice, your eye seems bright and eager, and the students look up at you with a touch of wondering admiration. Two types of teacher – in any kind

of education, but adult education is a specially dangerous area in these ways – should be particularly suspected: the charismatic, an imaginative pied piper of Hamelin; and the systems builder, an intellectual pied piper of Hamelin, who offers a complete guide and system to experience. Men who are a combination of both – some types of Marxist are like that – are the most dubious. Any teacher who begins to acquire fans, disciples, followers, ought to suspect himself until he has examined as honestly as he can the nature of these relationships. He may be getting between the students and their own hold on the subject. We should be glad to be judged by the degree to which our students stand on their own feet, out of our shadows. Which means we have to try to make sure they retain their freedom to be critical of us. Or, if that sounds too grand, ironic about us and towards us.[4]

A teacher talented in the dangerous hypnotic way Hoggart describes can easily turn his class into an audience for a personal performance. Often when students praise a teacher for being 'a good lecturer', what they mean is that he or she is a stimulating performer, by turns clown, tragedian, preacher, rhetorician, who rouses emotions at the time but leaves nothing for students to do themselves. Craft tutors can suffer the same sort of temptation to show off their expertise, only of course the 'performance' will take the form of a demonstration. In such cases a large part of the group's time will be taken up by a flawless demonstration by the teacher, which students are often quite happy to encourage.

The group is the wrong size

There are some basic laws of group life which relate to its size. The larger the group, the fewer the people who will speak. It runs roughly like this:

3–6 people: Everyone speaks.
7–10 people: Almost everyone speaks. Quieter people say less. One or two may not speak at all.

11–18 people: 5 or 6 people speak a lot, 3 or 4 others join in occasionally.

19–30 people: 3 or 4 people dominate.

30+ people: Little participation is possible.

A friend who is a distinguished adult educationist, with whom I discussed this phenomenon, told me that he had once been present at an international conference of 60 people. A lecture had been given by an eminent scientist who concluded by inviting questions from the floor. 'Do you know,' commented my friend, 'that the only three people who asked questions were *all* Nobel prize-winners!'

Here then is the simple explanation for non-participating behaviour in large groups: it takes far more courage to speak in a large than a small group. Here are the comments of first, a student nurse, and second, and MBA student:

I can talk in a group of four, I freeze in a group of ten!

It takes guts to join in a larger group discussion: there's that awful moment when out of the corner of your eye you see every face turned to yours. You feel everyone judging you, so the temptation is to stay mum.

The ideal size for a learning group is between 8 and 12. Anything smaller than 8 runs the risk that there will be too small a range of opinions and experiences. Increase the group much beyond 12 and you will inevitably find that it becomes difficult to draw everyone in.

Sometimes, however, you will find that you are landed with a larger group because administratively it is 'more convenient'. There are workable solutions to this problem.

I plan sessions which alternate whole-group talk/discussion with lots and lots of role-play in threes and fours.

I give a general introduction lasting 10 minutes, then I split the group into smaller groups of five or six with a problem to solve. They report back to the main group for the final 15 minutes.

Pairs working on mini projects, prepared in advance by
me . . .

Beware, though, of introducing small-group work without
designing it carefully and thinking it through:

My heart sinks at a conference or the like, when the session
leader says brightly, 'Now we're going to split into buzz
groups for five minutes' and gives you some entirely pointless 'task'. You know it's meant to encourage participation,
but so often it just seems a stale and meaningless device,
and sometimes, I'm sorry to say, suggests that the lecturer
can't be bothered to work out something better.

The room arrangement is inappropriate

The course venue was a small and hideous room in a hotel
with no natural light, striped wallpaper and noisy air con-
ditioning. You either shouted to make yourself heard over
the fans or turned it off and began to feel terrible through
lack of oxygen. We all had our elbows in each other's ribs
because it was so cramped. The ultimate irony was that the
course was on customer care!

The room was a great big barn: high ceilings, bare floor, hard
upright chairs. The only way to get people feeling more
comfortable was to set out our chairs in a circle in one corner.

Manipulating the physical shape of your group – where and
how participants sit – has an enormous influence on how they
behave. The key factors for maximum group contact and participation are:

- keep the space between chairs to a minimum;
- remove redundant chairs;
- establish open 'eyelines' – let everyone be able to see everyone else without having to twist or turn;
- comfortable but businesslike chairs;

- a room that just fits the group, not too big and not too small (but too small is better than too big);
- tables or desks that fit the purpose;
- thinking carefully about where you seat yourself.

There are hundreds of ways in everyday life in which the way we arrange and use the furniture in a situation is a symbolic way of showing how we feel in it, or of showing what the power and communication situation is. One chair round a dining table might have arms – it is a 'carver', and in many families this chair will always be taken by the most authoritative person and will be put at what becomes the head of the table. In most churches the parson's distinctive and influential role is stressed by the fact that he or she stands some distance apart from the congregation, who usually sit facing him or her in strict rows and are not expected to make any but a unanimous response. Quakers, on the other hand, who have no priest and who encourage contributions from anyone at a meeting, arrange their chairs in a hollow square with no special places. In an office one can expect the manager who leaves the desk to come and sit companionably beside a visitor to be friendlier than the manager who remains firmly behind it.

Exactly the same sort of symbolic representations are at work in learning groups. A group listening to a lecture will sit in straight rows facing a lecturer, who sits or stands apart. The arrangement of the chair emphasizes that the lecturer is a special person.

In a group where a little more discussion is expected, the tutor may still stand apart, but will face people sitting in two curved rows. In a craft group where the students are working individually and expect individual attention from the tutor, they will sit at tables dotted all over the room. Where they expect to help each other and work in small groups, several desks will be pushed together. In a discussion group where the tutor is no more than chairperson, the chairs might be arranged in a completely closed circle in which the tutor takes his or her place just like anyone else.

Desks and chairs themselves serve to emphasize roles and relationships. It is quite usual in most classrooms to find that the tutor's desk is larger and the chair more comfortable than the rest of the furniture in the room. It may be even perched on a platform – literally in a 'high up' place.

Tutors who abandon their chairs to stand in front of the desk, or perch on it, may be able to talk more informally with students. When they are behind desks they emphasize their teacher role. In a circular or hollow-square seating arrangement, tutors who want to emphasize that they are just another member will take care to leave the special chair alone. When they resume the role of leader they will return to it.

You are sure to find that a group tries to emphasize your role as leader by creating physical space between you and them:

> I always arrived first to set out exactly the right number of chairs in a neat circle. By the time we began, I nearly always found that, mysteriously, a space had appeared between my chair and my neighbours!

> I've noticed that people will go to considerable lengths to avoid sitting next to me. In one large group I teach, students will even form a second row rather than take the last 'free' spaces at either side of me.

It's up to you how you deal with this phenomenon. Let it pass unremarked if you feel it is of no significance, or even that it is a valuable way of emphasizing your leadership role. Insist on closing the gap if 'total equality' is your aim.

Comfortable and uncomfortable chairs, large and small groups have other inescapable influences. Infant-sized chairs, apart from being extremely uncomfortable, may suggest a childish role to a student. Hard, upright chairs may communicate an unpleasantly spartan and disciplined atmosphere. One of the most difficult groups I have ever had in adult education was in an open prison where I had been asked to bring my own class to form a discussion group with some pre-release prisoners. To add to our considerable nervous uncertainty of how to conduct ourselves in so unfamiliar a setting we had our first few meetings at one end of an enormous cold hut, sitting in a circle on hard wooden chairs, and generally gazing at our knees. Discussion was slow. The improvement when we moved to a small sitting-room with easy chairs was amazing. No doubt this was partly because we had by then been meeting for three weeks but the easy chairs in themselves seemed to suggest that we could all relax, and the social rather than educational associations were a positive advantage.

It does not need elaborate research (though there has been some) to show how influential the seating is on the kinds of communication people make and feel able to make. Clearly, sheer physical distance is important. Someone sitting at the back of a number of rows is less likely to speak to the lecturer than someone at the front. For people sitting at the front, the difficulties of twisting round to address other people or even to see and hear other people will generally mean that most people listen to and encourage talk from the one person who has a good view of everybody – the lecturer. In the opposite type of group, by sitting close to people and facing them, it is extremely hard not to talk to them, which is why contributions to conversation in a circle are usually divided pretty evenly between members. After only a short time the pattern becomes well known to all the members and very hard to break. The longer a lecture pattern continues, the harder it is for the shyest, most silent member to speak; the longer the garrulous 'circle' group continues, the harder it is for them to listen to a lecture. In other words, the shape of the setting first influences and then reinforces the typical way in which the class behaves.

You should feel free to manipulate the teaching space in any way you like, altering it frequently if necessary during each group meeting.

The students resist

I once sat in on an industrial relations course with a group of 18 men who were using an elegant room well equipped for small-group work, with special tables and close carpeting to deaden noise. The small-group discussion came at the end of a tiring day's work which consisted mostly of listening to lectures, with half an hour for discussion afterwards. It was clear that in their three small groups they were feeling disgruntled and felt that they were groping for direction, even though they dutifully exchanged experiences and all spoke a great deal. After several weeks of going along with the tutor they asked for whole-group discussion, as they said they felt they could benefit more from the exchange of views among the whole group than they could in groups of six. Perhaps this was a more ambiguous situation than it at first appeared: the tutor was taking no part at all in the small-group work, but spent this part of the class 'writing up notes' (having a rest). Neither was there any reporting-back session. The afternoon ended when the small groups broke up. The participants made their dissatisfaction clear. The tutor didn't seem to care, so why should they? Maybe their attempt to resume whole-group work, which involved the tutor becoming group leader again, was simply a way of trying to force the tutor to do his job.

If your group pleads for 'lectures' then clearly you must take the request seriously as a sign that something is wrong with the structure, method or content of the course. Don't leap into delivery of a lecture without a careful analysis of where the problem lies. Listen attentively to what the group has to say, bracing yourself for critical comments. The most appropriate solution will depend on the cause of the problem:

My group didn't like 'participation'. The underlying reason was that they all lacked confidence. I had pitched the opening level of the course too high. By stepping back three stages, we solved the problem and they began to join in.

Real cause – no experience of discussion. Had to have lots of patience, lots of silence, lots of coaxing . . . then it worked.

. . . lack of proper motivation . . . people being sent on training courses because no one knew what else to do with them. A few days away from base at a nice country house was regarded as a good chance for a rest – sitting back and 'listening to lectures'. The only way to change that was to alter the recruitment policy by insisting that the delegates were purposefully chosen, well-briefed, and turned up knowing exactly what was expected of them.

What makes a good tutor?

Many of the problems cropping up in groups come down in the end to the personality and skills of the tutor. Thinking back to my own schooldays and to the teaching I have encountered since, the outstanding teachers all shared an enthusiastic, open, relaxed style while teaching. Away from the classroom or training room they were people of very different personality. Educational research has confirmed what most of us already know from this kind of personal experience – that effective tutors have these characteristics:

- a warm personality – ability to show approval and acceptance of students;
- social skill – ability to weld the group together and control it without dominating it;
- an 'indirect' manner of teaching which generates and uses learners' ideas;
- organizing ability so that resources are booked, administration is smoothly handled;
- skill in spotting and resolving learner problems;
- enthusiasm – for instance, an animated demeanour, plenty of eye contact, varied voice inflexion;
- creative ability to generate innovative ways of presenting ideas and skills;
- courage to stand up for what is right;
- the ability to encourage risk-taking where people push their personal boundaries;
- willingness to challenge; ability to present ideas and options which encourage learners to do more than they thought possible and to look again at their cherished assumptions;
- resilience in the face of stress;
- presence – a natural authority and ease;
- clarity in simplifying the complex, but without over-simplifying.

There is no identikit way that these qualities will play out in any individual tutor. It is not a one-size-fits-all approach, but here is one way it can look to the grateful participant:

She just plunged into the work of teaching us...inexhaustible energy on our behalf. Knew our problems before we'd seen them coming ourselves and helped us find the solution that was right for us...cared passionately about our progress. Loved her subject and was extremely knowledgeable in it, yet gave us all the feeling that we were experts in it too because all our efforts were bent towards our *finding out for ourselves*. Magically we always had everything to hand – books, tapes, reference material. Her husband once told me that she came home every single day utterly exhausted and threw herself on the sofa unable to speak for half an hour. I must say I wasn't surprised – we had drained her dry!

This is the sort of person who makes a naturally good teacher, but it is a style which cannot be faked. Some sage and experienced adult educationists will say that they believe in behaving as if one is transparent with a class, because one is always more transparent than one realizes. These are wise words for any teacher, but they are particularly appropriate for those who teach adults.

Chapter **4**

▶ Mixed ability groups

It is a mistake to assume that *mixed ability* inevitably means there will be problems. Most of the leadership development courses I now run inevitably have people of very mixed ability and it is rarely if ever a problem. As a learner myself, I had a vivid experience of how little difference it can make. I put myself on a course about coaching run in a horrible hotel just off the M1. I had very low expectations of the course. The tutors were American and it seemed likely to be full of Californian jargon. Since at the stage I did the course I had been doing coaching for ten years or more, I also felt it was unlikely that I would learn very much. When the first round of introductions was in full swing I began to feel even more depressed and was quite prepared to depart early. Probably about half the people on the course had no coaching experience whatsoever and the majority of the others were counsellors or therapists – a related but different skill (see Chapter 10). However, I stayed, and it was one of the best courses I have ever attended – as a course junkie, I have attended a lot. The reasons were that the course was entirely participative. It allowed people to enter at their own level. It mattered not a jot that some people had no experience and some had a lot. Where it covered ground I already knew well, I simply felt affirmed. Where it covered unfamiliar ground I felt stretched and challenged.

All groups of learners are of mixed ability to some extent. Even members of an apparently homogeneous group will still

actually vary a good deal in their individual talents and interests. Nevertheless, for teachers of adults, there are often startling
and obvious variations in ability, age and previous educational
experience. These can pose apparently intractable problems:

> At least in school you can be sure of one thing – the chil-
> dren in each class are all the same age, and in our school
> they come from virtually identical social backgrounds since
> we are a neighbourhood school on a large pre-war hous-
> ing estate. It amazed me to see the very same classrooms at
> night when I took my first adult class. It was the only
> 'Beginner's Woodwork' for some miles, so people drove con-
> siderable distances to attend. I expected my class to be all
> men, but of course there were women as well – that was the
> first shock. Second surprise, some of the class were clearly
> very well educated and had plenty of money, some were a
> bit down at heel, the eldest was in her seventies, and the
> youngest was a kid of 18 I'd known when he was at the
> school as a pupil. I'd prepared a lesson on a simple joint,
> but I could see by the end of the two hours that I'd some-
> how got it all wrong. Several had never even seen a chisel
> before, or didn't know how to measure, while there were
> three or four who were expecting to get on with making big
> projects – a rocking chair in one case and a bed in another,
> and seemed to know a lot of the basics already. One of the
> main difficulties was having men and women in the same
> class. All the men had at least done some woodwork before,
> but not one of the women had. I worried about it for weeks,
> but in the end the problem solved itself. All but one of the
> women stopped coming, and I was left with a core of 12
> reasonably adept regulars. I can't say I felt happy about it,
> but what could I have done?

The situation looks even less satisfactory when seen from the
student's view:

> When it was clear that my marriage was on the rocks, I
> decided that I had to update my skills, so I went on a word

processing course run by a private company in the town. I was just about able to type with two fingers, but I'd never had any proper typing training. The brochure said this didn't matter. Unfortunately it did. There were 11 other people on the course. Some of them were very fast, skilled typists whose companies had sent them for updating – I don't know why, as quite a few seemed to have used a computer before. One was a freelance journalist who'd just bought a computer and couldn't work out how to use it, then there were two or three people like me. The tutor's method was to give a lot of instructions all at once at the beginning of each section, then to set us all the same exercise. It was hopeless. The experienced people rattled away. Because they could type accurately they made fewer mistakes (so they didn't have to use the 'Delete' key much!) and finished first. She timed the exercises by these fast people and just said 'oh never mind, just do what you can' to the rest of us. It was utterly baffling and very discouraging: I felt very stupid. Since I was paying, I stuck it out, but it was a waste of money. Several of the other people thought the same. I noticed that the company closed down a few months later, so perhaps the word spread that they weren't much good.

Giving in to the deadly attraction of gearing everything to the needs of the most able learners was only one of the traps this tutor dug for herself. The other traps included a failure to recognize that a class of a very mixed ability means a need for a completely different approach. This tutor at least kept her class with her to the end, perhaps because they were desperate to learn and had all parted with good money. They clung to the hope that there might be an improvement, in spite of evidence to the contrary. Where classes are cheap, or the students' need is not so great, it is often simpler (as it was with the woodwork class) for the students simply to melt away:

As tutor-in-charge I became very worried about the social anthropology group. It started with 45 enrolments, and was down to 8 by Christmas. I looked first at the enrolment cards and saw immediately what a problem [the tutor] had – graduates, two PhDs, lots of 'ordinary' housewives, several under-twenties with no O levels . . . I visited the class as a preliminary to closing it down. It was clear that he'd made it all much much worse through his own inexperience. He didn't know anybody's name (and they didn't seem to know his). He muttered into lecture notes he seemed to be *reading* all the time. Participation was nil. Even so the surviving students appeared to be getting something out of it and begged us to let the class continue. We refused but I made sure the tutor attended our next training day.

The problems, then, are the ones I have already touched on in previous chapters. Unless the class is for some reason an unusually specialized one, it may contain students of mixed ability. Their ages may range over the whole adult spectrum. They will bring with them an astonishing variety of experience and confidence. Their reasons for coming to the class will vary, and so will their expectations. Some may be very clever, some will seem moderately able, some may have little apparent ability.

Like any difficulty in teaching there are no instant, pat solutions. However, there are several possible approaches which can help.

Administration

Some tutors are too new to teaching to realize that they are being asked to deal with an impossibly difficult group. Some of the problems of mixed ability teaching are in fact caused by inept administration. No teacher should be left unsupported to face a group 45 strong, like the social anthropology teacher described above whose supervisor eventually came to his rescue, but far too late.

It is true that sometimes an organizer or commissioner of learning must knowingly run the risk of offering something general when the subject itself demands something more specialized. However, one way of coping with mixed ability groups is to take preventive action beforehand by making it perfectly clear to prospective participants what is on offer.

Let's take a computer course as an example and imagine how the failed course described earlier might be publicized. The briefer the description, the more likely it is to raise unrealistic hopes or to encourage a reader to read whatever assumptions they care to into vague words:

> Word Processing for Beginners. One-week course starts on first Mondays in the month.

Compare this with:

> Word Processing for beginners. This is a three-day intensive course for competent typists (60–80 wpm) who want to learn how to use Windows. We assume you have no previous experience of using a mouse. We will train you in using Microsoft Office. The emphasis is on Word, but we will also introduce you to spreadsheets and databases. By the end of the course you should be able to use all the main menu functions, including print, mail merge, tables and formatting. We will also introduce you to Draw. (There is a more advanced course for PowerPoint.)

The first entry tells a prospective student little. It gives no indication of the previous experience expected and no hint of the pace, style and final accomplishments of its graduates. It is the type of description written by people who want to hedge their bets: they are afraid enrolments will go down if they are too specific.

The second entry is a good deal more helpful. It identifies the entry level expected, is specific about objectives and makes it clear that there will be a brisk and business-like pace to the proceedings. This realistic approach will certainly discourage the people for whom the course is not intended, but then if they did enrol they would quickly find out for themselves that the course was unsuitable. 'Enrolment at any price' in practice means enrolment at the cost of student achievement and satisfaction and a high price also paid in tutor frustration.

Entry

Think carefully about how prospective learners make further decisions as to whether your event is for them or not. How you contact them is vital. If you are running one-off events, all your communications with your learners will be telling them something about you. Make sure it is the message you want to convey. For instance, if they have to wait weeks to hear whether or not they have a place, this will not give a good impression. If you work in adult education be wary of any organization which still has the old-style September-rush enrolment queues heralding the start of the new academic year, and does not seem to have heard of the telephone, let alone the Internet.

Encourage direct communication. In my company, when we run events for commissioning employers, we always refine the target profile with the client, asking him or her to discourage people who fall outside it. We also ask for a list of names and phone numbers. Where it is a new event and we feel we don't know enough about our target group, we will always ring a sample of people and ask them:

- What do you already know about X subject?
- What are you hoping to learn?
- What's your reason for wanting to go on the course?

If it's clear that someone is over- or under-qualified for an event, we will always discuss it thoroughly with them, suggesting an alternative event if we feel that only disappointment could result from attending our event. Similarly, when we send out joining instructions, we encourage people to contact us with their queries or worries. A surprising number do so. Even where the question is something like 'I've got to go to a meeting on the second day, is that all right?' we will take the opportunity to confirm that this person is in our target group.

It is good practice to let people have as much information in advance as possible. At a minimum this should include:

- the objectives for the event;
- an outline programme;

- your CV;
- the kinds of method you will be using;
- dress code;
- telephone number for the venue and directions about how to get there;
- any equipment or other materials they need to bring with them.

Sensitive entry processes and well-written descriptions of what to expect can do a lot to head off some of the problems of a mixed ability class.

Most of us are actually rather good at self-selection, as long as we are given enough information to form a judgement. These tactics will also help you because you will then have details on your learners.

However, in spite of all this care, you may still find yourself in difficulties. A well-attested story tells how a visitor to one class was baffled by the large cards he noticed propped on every student's table. Each card had a different label. One said 7.15, another 7.35, another 7.50, and so on. When he inquired what the cards signified, he was told, 'Oh, that's when Mrs ___ comes round to give us our individual teaching!' History does not relate what the class was supposed to do during the rest of the time it met. In other words this tutor had assumed that the only way her students could learn was by demonstration by herself on a one-to-one basis. Although few tutors would evolve such an extraordinary solution to their problem, very many behave as if they believe it to be true that students can only learn when a teacher is overtly 'teaching', either by concentrating on one-to-one relationships, or by addressing the group as a whole. There will, of course, always be some occasions when one or other of these methods is the most appropriate, but there can be little justification for using either one of them all the time.

In a two-hour session with 20 students, allowing a few minutes for a coffee break and a few more for setting up equipment, if each student were to receive an equal amount of time this would only come to about four and a half minutes each. The bold students store up their queries, the shy ones say little. For most students, their exclusive time with the teacher is too short for more than a cursory inspection and general encouragement; jealous suspicions of 'favouritism' develop, and students also become far too dependent on the tutor when the aim of the tutor ought to be to encourage them towards independence.

Classroom solutions

It *is* possible to teach mixed ability groups successfully. Here is one teacher who met the challenge:

> I started my method several years ago when I had a dress-making class where complete beginners and advanced students were all mixed up together. It was impossible to find one topic to suit everybody. I felt I wanted to give most time to the beginners, but there was also a need to persuade the advanced people to be more adventurous.
>
> I began by preparing handwritten photocopied sheets of instructions and drawings to go with sets of small pieces of fabric already cut out from my own scrap box. I seem to remember that this first exercise was a quite difficult one on pin tucking and seaming, a topic several students had been enquiring about but had been too timid to attempt. I suggested that each week we might spend half an hour on a similar project, then the rest of the time they could continue their own work. I explained that everything they needed to know to produce perfect work was contained on the sheet and that they had no need of me for explanations except in emergencies.
>
> There were some long faces at first but the method seemed to succeed more or less straight away. Since each member of the group had a different fabric they naturally achieved different effects which caused a lot of useful discussion in which the students learned from each other. (I make a point of encouraging informal discussion. I always join them for this as I feel it is here that the class is really learning.)
>
> More and more time was taken up on the 'experimental' work. It eventually spread out over the next year to designing

their own clothes. The confidence given by learning on their own to master some of the most intricate techniques in dressmaking spread to the clothes they made for themselves and their children, which were creditably adventurous in design and execution.

The beginners began to feel left out so I was soon using the method with everybody. The duplicated sheets needed alteration – some proved too detailed, others too scanty – and were also too flimsy for constant use. The next lot were nicely typed and mounted on plastic card. At one stage I was nearly put back in the old situation. So much excitement, so many queries came that I almost could not cope. I started filing the worksheets in expanding document cases, compiling loose-leaf folders of reference material, card indexes and later on colour slides to which the class themselves constantly contributed and referred and to which they were directed by each week's work cards. Advanced students helped prepare material for beginners and one gradually builds up a stock of first-class material.

This was a radical solution. The reason it worked so well was that the tutor shifted the emphasis from herself as the fount of all information to a set of alternative resources. Although these were designed and indeed controlled by her, the students were not dependent on her verbally-given expertise during class time. Careful preparation meant that she could cope comfortably with both beginners and experienced learners in the same group.

If this idea sounds familiar, of course it is. It has been perfected in the UK over 45 years by the best primary schoolteachers. The end of the old 'eleven plus' freed primary schools from the need to stream and label children in order to get the ablest 20 per cent through the narrow gates of the exam. This freedom meant developing methods such as projects, group work and resource-based learning in classes where the most able could learn side by side with the least able without any loss of motivation in either. The outward symbol of this shift has been the change in the way children sit. In the old-style primary school, children sat in rows because they all needed a clear view of the teacher. Today, they sit round tables in groups of four or five. Because examinations dominate the secondary curriculum, the old format still holds, and the chairs once more all face the same way. This is one of the many unpleasant shocks that children experience when they make the primary–secondary transfer.

Successful teaching of adult mixed ability groups almost always involves applying the same techniques that work so well with young children: breaking away from one-pace, one-resource teaching, and moving towards flexibly-paced, multi-resourced learning.

I would not wish to claim that this is simple to carry off successfully. It takes more preparation, more organizational skill and probably more flair than traditional teaching. It has often been said about primary-school methods that a 'weak' teacher's deficiencies were more easily hidden under a talk-and-chalk method and rigid discipline whereas they are mercilessly exposed with 'modern' approaches.

However, a mixed ability group leaves you with little option but to plump for a flexible, resource-based approach, assuming, that is, that you want all your students to learn from the course.

The solution to the teaching problems of the computer course would be to apply these same techniques: for instance, to put all the instructions and exercises onto disk for use on each machine, backed up by a simple manual, and to encourage the learners to work through these disks at their own pace. The tutor then becomes a resource for problem-solving and explanation to anyone in difficulties. This would be much more likely to allow people of very mixed ability to work happily together.

Objectives

I just have an idea in my head of where I want to get to by the end of the course . . . no, I never write it down.

(Catering tutor)

My aim is to turn them into critical, sensitive readers.
(Literature tutor)

Turn them into better managers!
(Management development tutor)

These vague and hopeful statements could well have described my own actual practice in my early days as a teacher, though of course I would have been as capable as anyone of writing down fine-sounding words had one of Her Majesty's Inspectors happened to call.

Today I am a reformed character. I would not dream of planning a piece of teaching or training without first making a proper list of objectives. The reasons are that making such a list helps me plan the syllabus, choose appropriate teaching methods, and usefully reminds me of how little it is actually possible to achieve in the limited time available to me for the course. It also helps me to define who the course is *for*, thus again anticipating and perhaps deflecting any problems of gross extremes in the abilities of my students.

It is useful to distinguish between 'aims' and 'objectives'. 'Aims' tends to describe the pious hopes that some teachers have of their learners, or that principals often claim for their institutions:

Our aim is to produce the leaders of tomorrow.

We aim to produce young adults who can reach their full potential intellectually, socially and physically.

'Objectives' are much more precise because they list the intended *outcomes* of the learning by stating what a person who completes the course should be able to do.

I find it useful to plan objectives by taking a step-by-step approach, consisting of formulating answers to a number of questions. The first of these is: 'Who are the participants?' I write an identikit portrait for myself, trying to answer these questions:

- What sort of people are they?
- What do they *want* to achieve from the course?
- What do they *need* to learn from it?
- What might stand in their way?

- What previous knowledge do they have of the subject?
- Why are they coming?

For instance, let's imagine I am mulling over how to fulfil a commission to run a series of courses for junior staff on how to run meetings. The answers to my own questions in this case run something like this:

Typical participant for course on 'running meetings'

Age about 30, woman, senior secretary or junior researcher. Wants more confidence to speak up at internal and external meetings; for the future, needs to know how to chair, write agenda and notes. Standing in the way currently: lack of assertiveness, lack of practice in leadership. Plenty of previous knowledge of attending meetings, very little of running them. Wants this training because she can see it is necessary for career advancement.

Writing this analysis helps me be clear in my own mind about who the course is for. When my client circulates the details throughout the organization, it will be as clear as possible to them who the course is for. If bogus beginners come forward (this is people who I discover or know have quite a lot of experience already) I have various options: to discourage them or arrange a more suitable piece of training; to find out what lies underneath this apparent miscasting; to accept them and use them as deliberate sources of advice and experience during the course. The point is that I can make the choice: there might be something to be said for any of these tactics. If I end up with a mixed ability class, then it is because I have weighed up the advantages and disadvantages myself: I am not helplessly accepting someone else's judgement.

Second, what do I want them to be able to do by the time they have completed the course? The key word here is 'do'. The ideal objective is one where the learner could *demonstrate competence to somebody else*, so words like 'understand' or 'appreciate' do not make for useful objectives because no two people could ever agree on what constitutes 'understanding' or 'appreciation'. For instance, 'understanding the role of computers in society' could mean anything from being able to name a single multinational computer company to being able to design an acceptable IT system for that same company. 'Appreciate the music of Beethoven' might mean anything from quite liking the final movement of the Ninth Symphony to being able to make fine judgements between the performances of two great orchestras playing that symphony.

It is better to stick to objectives where the learner's achievements by the end of the course begin with words like:

make	identify
plan	compare
list	solve
produce	write

For my course on running meetings, my objectives given to the participants will probably look something like this:

By the end of the two-day course you should be able to:

- write an agenda for a two-hour meeting;
- prepare briefing notes for participants, if necessary;
- chair a meeting of up to seven people;
- write and circulate notes on the meeting.

Third, by what standard would I judge whether students had reached the objective? Here, again, it helps to be specific. In the jargon, it is necessary to add 'performance criteria'. Suppose the aim is to teach someone to deflea their cat. The objective could be stated as: 'By the time X has completed this piece of learning, they should be able to deflea their cat successfully'. Ah, yes, but what constitutes 'success'? Is it a success if the cat stops scratching for a day? Is it successful if you can't see any fleas with the naked eye?

The objective will be even more helpful if it runs like this:

By the time X has completed this piece of learning, they should be able to deflea their cat so that when the cat is combed with a fine metal comb five days later, no live fleas or larvae are seen on the comb.

The virtue of this much more long-winded version is that it would be perfectly possible for X to prove that they could indeed deflea a cat competently. Furthermore, the same criteria could be widely applied and judged.

If I apply this same rule to my objectives for the 'running meetings' course, then I also need to add 'performance criteria'. For instance to my objective on 'writing notes', I could add: 'write and circulate notes of the meeting *which are accepted by participants as a succinct but accurate record*'.

Ideally, objectives also need to state in what circumstances the objective is being applied. For instance, for my learners, it would not be fair to expect them to chair a large and tricky negotiating meeting involving outsiders, so my objectives should probably also contain a conditional phrase such as 'Given an intra-departmental meeting of not more than ten people, could write and circulate notes which are accepted by participants as a succinct but accurate record'.

Summing up, then, a good objective will state:

- what the learner can *do*;
- under what *conditions* the learner will perform;
- to what *standard*.

Finally, who else needs to be consulted? Once you have an outline list of objectives, it is always a good idea to seek opinions on them. If you are working in an organization, then consult the relevant line managers or your commissioning client. Are these the skills they want their trainees to have? Ask the learners too – is this what they think they want and need? Ask people who have done the same kind of course in the past. Most objectives have to be modified at least a little in the light of this exercise.

Writing objectives takes time and care, but it is effort well spent. It forces you to focus on what it is actually possible for people to learn in the time available, and will help you decide where you should put the boundaries on previous experience or ability in your learners. It will also help you choose the most appropriate teaching methods. If one of my objectives is that people should be able to chair a meeting, then clearly I must spend large chunks of the course giving everyone practice at doing just that, which immediately suggests a heavy emphasis on role-play.

Teaching a mixed ability group can be a blessing or a misfortune. Which it turns out to be is, to a large extent, in your own hands. If the needs of your subject and the standard to which it must be taught dictate homogeneity, then you (or your administrators) need to be both honest and ruthless at the recruitment stage. If this is neither possible nor desirable, then the best solutions will lie in the direction of the kinds of learning which are the subjects of several subsequent chapters in this book. In general, the more participatory the method, the easier it is for people of all abilities to learn from the same experience:

> The previous Minister had been a rather intense academic theologian, and 'Bible study' had dwindled under his leadership to a tiny cohort of people who could keep up with his high-level dissertations. When he left, the new Minister was much more interested in lay participation and a system of 'house groups' grew and flourished. The extraordinary thing about this is how mixed they are: all ages, all abilities, yet even the more timid and really quite unacademic people have taken part and have even led the discussions. This is because the whole thing is based on *everyone* taking part. I have been at evenings where a PhD in theology has clearly got as much out of it as a new young member from the local housing estate. That's because the leadership training has been very thorough, and because we have relied on excellent videos and discussion papers and because the emphasis has been on being able to join in discussion at any level of experience or knowledge.

Chapter 5

▶ The first session

The first session is important. This is true whether it is the first session of a single day's event, the first meeting of an adult education class or the opening hour of a week-long course. It is in this session that vital first impressions are formed and motivation built on or crushed:

> The organization ran a series of workshops for about 80 people at a time to explain the changes that were being introduced. The first session always consisted of a senior manager giving a welcome talk. The word went round about how hostile the audiences were and it was hard to persuade anyone to do the talk. I was organizing the conference centre where it all happened and I was acutely aware of what a difference this opening piece made. I saw dozens and dozens of them. The manager who could be relaxed, be straightforward and honest about what was going on, keep it short, make a few jokes – not too many, mind – always meant a much better day. Where we had the reverse, the day was finished before it had even started.

> The first night of the pottery class we didn't do anything at all, we just sat there while he gave us the whole history of clay. This wasn't what I'd wanted at all. He just talked and talked and talked.

The participants may be feeling nervous, but it is you who are on trial, not they. Even after many years of running courses and learning events of all kinds, I still feel a quiver of apprehension before meeting any new group. What will they be like? Will they like me? Will it go well? Are my assumptions about what they want and need accurate? Am I up to it? Have I got enough material? This apprehension is probably a healthy sign. I have heard actors say the same thing – that some stage fright means you give a better performance than when you feel none. Personally, I know that the day I routinely feel no tightening at all of the stomach muscles before meeting a new group will be the day that I decide it's time to stop.

This aerobics teacher describes well what the first session needs:

I think of the first meeting as a kind of first date with a desirable partner who has to be wooed and courted. Shyness is out on my part while I have to recognize it on theirs. I mustn't be too overwhelming, but on the other hand I have to make what is on offer seem attractive. If it isn't a success, I know they'll disappear – endless polite excuses, but I won't see them again! Since they pay on each occasion and I get a cut, it matters to my wallet as well as to my pride . . .

Adults are rightly choosy. Whether it comes out of your pocket or out of an employer's budget doesn't seem to matter too much. If we don't like what we're getting, we will stay away or leave. Your plan to avoid this humiliating debacle will fall naturally into three phases: before, during and after.

Before the first session

This is the research phase. Find out as much as you can in advance about who will be in the group. Whenever I can, I will phone people in advance. This serves a number of purposes. First, it helps me cope with any nervousness I might be feeling, because when you actually talk to the people they almost inevitably come across as helpful, pleasant and friendly. Second, it is good customer care. It shows that you are interested enough in participants' needs to take the trouble to contact them. Third and most important, it gives me vital information about what they expect and want. I always take notes during these conversations.

The questions I recommend are dead simple:

- *What can you tell me about why you are attending this event?* The answers here are always revealing. The question gives the sceptics the chance to voice their scepticism without feeling judged. It allows the enthusiasts to be enthusiastic. It also allows for occasional blinding honesty – the people who confess that they don't really know, but it's a week away from the office and they're looking forward to it.

- *What do you want to get out of it?* Replies here will tell you what people feel they must achieve. If you feel that these aims are over-ambitious, this is the time to say so. If, as is more usual, they are over-modest, this is also the time to say so.

- *What do you already know about the subject?* Or you can ask this question a slightly different way: *What other training or development have you done in this area?* This question gives you the chance to assess where people are in their learning. For instance, if you are running something suitable for beginners, you may well realize by asking this question that you have a bogus beginner in the group – someone who has already covered much of the territory you will be exploring. If so, probe their reasons for doing the same material all over again. Lack of confidence is the usual explanation. Where you feel that a participant is likely to be either bored or out of their depth, now is the time to say so, suggesting an alternative event or course.

- *What reservations do you have?* Note the way this question is asked. Not *Do you have any reservations?* Asking a question that begins *do*, *don't*, *is* or *isn't* will inevitably produce the answer the listener thinks you want to hear – in this case, 'No'. Asking *what* reservations assumes that everyone is likely to have some, which is indeed the case. You need to know what these are. Common replies might be

> None that need trouble you!
> Afraid it will be a waste of time.
> Nervous about looking silly.

Worried about my in-tray and what will happen while I'm out of the office.

Hope we're not going to do role-play because I hate it!

- *What else would it be useful for me to know?* This final question is immensely useful. By this stage of the conversation there is usually some trust and friendliness. Some people will say that there is nothing else you need to know. Others will use the moment to give you important additional information. In one such set of conversations I was told about the recent termination of a pregnancy and the agonizing guilt that this event had created, the death of a parent, a phobia about beef and a deadly quarrel some years back with a participant who was also going to be on the course.

Sorting out the housekeeping

Some years ago, I joined a course which met at our local concrete university. The first class was scheduled to start at 7.00 p.m. Unfortunately, the signposting at reception was inscrutable and the building itself designed to confuse, its grimy towers being linked by windswept ramps. I finally found the room after 15 minutes of searching, but alas! The venue had been changed. A notice flapped on the open door announcing a different room (one I had passed several times already in my search). The tutor gave me a hostile stare as I climbed over benches to find a seat. He was annoyed because his introductory chat was being interrupted so many times by similarly lost latecomers – indeed they kept sliding in until 7.45.

The course was not a success. Even though most people's fees were, like mine, being paid by their employers, the initial group of 22 were down to 10 by the fourth meeting.

Most such problems are entirely preventable by attentive housekeeping and good customer care:

- inform the receptionist;
- make sure he or she is welcoming;
- direct people with clear signage;

- double check the room booking;
- double check any audio-visual equipment.
- Arrange the room so that it suits your purposes (see also pages 70 to 73).

Advance information to learners

Sometimes people just turn up on the spot and you can have no way of knowing in advance who they are. More commonly you will know. The more you can let them know about the event in advance, the better it will be for you and for them. Think about sending people any or all of the following:

- a welcome letter;
- a course outline;
- a description of the methods you are going to use;
- a map with instructions for finding the venue;
- food arrangements;
- additional costs, if any;
- dress code information;
- details of any equipment they need to buy or bring with them;
- reading lists;
- book list;
- brief CVs of tutors.

The more information people have about you, the methods, the content and what is expected of them, the fewer their shocks will be on the day and the better it will be all round.

Make a plan

You may feel that a plan is too formal, but I believe it helps. If you have a plan you can always abandon it if you wish, but without one, you are likely to feel unanchored and apprehensive. The simplest plan has three columns for time, activity and materials. Be realistic. Most activities will take longer than you think.

During the event

The first few minutes

The most useful comparison is to think of yourself as a host. A good host greets people warmly, introduces them to each other and tries to make sure that everyone has a pleasant time. Unfortunately, it is all too easy to fall short of this ideal:

> Got to the group on time, but no tutor to be seen – she arrived five minutes late, puffing and panting, but with no apology!

> We sat there in silence and semi-darkness – very uncomfortable. On the dot of ten, the tutor walked in, switched on another light and launched straight into a lecture. I had no idea who the other people were. In fact the tutor never told us his name either.

A better tactic is to arrive in plenty of time – at least 20 minutes before the official start time. Greet people warmly, ask their names, and introduce them to one another.

Introducing yourself

Always say something about yourself at the formal beginning of any event. A full length biography is not what is required, but some information about you is essential. It need only take a minute or two, but should include:

- your name;
- your passion for your subject;
- your aims for the event;
- how you got from your original career to this event;
- what your credentials are – your authority for teaching the subject at all.

The swiftest and one of the most effective introductions I ever see of this sort is given by an actor with whom I frequently work. It takes about a minute and her intro goes like this:

Hello, my name is X [first and surname]. I'm passionate about the whole subject of helping people give better presentations because I see all the time what a difference it can make to how we communicate. My aim today is to help you improve your presentation style and confidence. I started as an actor in the theatre and TV but now I do almost exclusively corporate work – I've been in it for six years, working with senior people in all sorts of sectors and industries. I specialize in working with people on their voices and I'm really looking forward to working with you today.

Learning people's names

If appropriate, have name badges prepared with people's names in letters big enough to be read easily at a distance – by you and by the participants. Never underestimate the importance of learning and using people's names as a way of making them feel that they matter to you and are part of the group. Not doing this is one of the main ways a group can fail:

A colleague and I were running a course we have been doing for some time, so I suppose it was running the risk of seeming a bit stale – to us that is. We were preoccupied on this occasion by some personal stuff – we were planning the launch of another course, very exciting and new and potentially very lucrative. Somehow we got very bound up in this and I think conveyed to the group that we were a bit over-pleased with ourselves. It was a big group, but normally I never have any trouble remembering people's names. This time I did. There were lots of women there of similar age and with very similar names: two Caroles, two Karens, a Caroline and a Carmel and we both kept getting them mixed up. We had very disappointing feedback from the group and thinking it over afterwards we both came to the conclusion that we had failed at this very basic level of acknowledging each individual.

There are a number of ruses you can use to help remember names in a big group:

- draw a seating plan for yourself and label each person as they introduce themselves;
- attach a private mnemonic to each person;
- use their names as early as possible and as often as possible.

Ice-breakers

Ice-breakers really help. They are vital for many reasons.

They oblige everyone to speak. Unless you speak you will not feel you are fully present at the event and all tutors want their participants to feel and be fully present, as no one can learn unless they are fully present. They help people get over the shy stage as quickly as possible, and they help *form* the group – people begin to get to know each other.

Depending on which ice-breakers you use, you can find out further vital information about what the group wants and expects.

There are literally thousands of possible ice-breakers. Indeed, there are whole books devoted to them. Most experienced tutors collect them from one another and as they see them used at events they attend as learners. What you choose will depend on how much time you have available – a longer course needs a more cohesive group so it will be worth a bigger investment of time. It will also depend on the subject. A solemn subject – a day's seminar on employment law, for instance – will not easily lend itself to a light-hearted ice-breaker. One important point about ice-breakers is that you should join in yourself. Never ask the group to do something where you remain aloof.

Here are some ideas for ice-breakers. They all work for me and may for you:

- Asking people to sit in alphabetical order of first names and then to introduce themselves to the group. This obliges everyone to exchange names and also to move – both excellent tactics.
- Asking people to introduce themselves and then to sit in date order according to when they started their present job. Once

sat down again, people introduce their neighbours. Works for similar reasons to above.

- Getting people to mingle as at a cocktail party. Ask them to find two other people with whom they have something in common and then to introduce each other to the rest of the group.
- Working in pairs, 'snowballing' to quartets. Ask people to state what they want from the event, and what they don't want, and then present to the rest of the group.
- Asking everyone to find an adjective that starts with the same letter as their first name and which also says something about their current state of mind or body, and then to introduce themselves to the rest of the group. For instance, *Hoarse Helen* had a very bad cold, and *Jolly John* was feeling relaxed.
- Asking people to state their names, jobs and what they would be doing if they were independently wealthy and had no need to work. This is fun and memorable. I saw this ice-breaker done on a course for the senior partners of a world famous accountancy firm and several people replied that they were already independently wealthy and what they were doing was the job they loved!
- Forming people into birth order groups (first child, only children and so on) and asking them to discuss and then report on what being in that birth order has done for their approach to whatever the subject of the course is.

Even the notorious 'creeping death' can work in some circumstances. This is the ice-breaker where you start at one side of the room and work your way around with everyone saying their names and something about themselves. It's called 'creeping death' because most people are so nervous before speaking that they don't hear any of their predecessors and are so relieved afterwards that they don't concentrate on what follows either. However, there is sometimes a place even for this oldie. I saw it used very effectively on an event attended by 120 people. The young American speaker/tutor asked people to 'laser' their contributions – i.e. keep them very short, and ruthlessly interrupted the first few people who showed signs of droning on. Most people quickly got the point and spoke for ten seconds or less. It was fun, involving and did the job surprisingly well.

Helping students relax

Ice-breakers will usually help people relax, but you need to keep in mind that people may still be feeling apprehensive. Getting them to own up to the apprehension is always a useful tactic and you can achieve this by asking the question directly: 'Who is feeling nervous here?' Or, 'How are you feeling about this event?' Naming the fear usually means taming the fear.

Introducing some laughter and pace is your next best tactic, depending of course on you and your personality and confidence. It takes a lot of experience to match the inspired clowning and energy of this enormously successful teacher of English as a foreign language, working with nervous and wary people of hugely mixed nationalities in a North London community centre:

> We plunge right in at the first class. My main idea is to make them laugh at me. Anyone can understand action jokes even if they have no English so I'm constantly acting the jokes. I ask them their names and perhaps say a few words in their languages – Urdu, Spanish, Greek, Bengali – they usually understand and correct me.
>
> I always make sure that we do a lot on the first night, but it's usually very simple things like prepositions – under, over, in, out. To teach these things I get under the table, go out of the door, stand on the chair and get people to say 'She's under the table', 'She's on the chair'.
>
> I always have plenty of real things to hand – bread, big jars of sweets – and we make up sentences about them: 'It's a sweet', 'It's a loaf'. By the end of the class, I make sure everyone has spoken at least once; usually I try to see that they've asked and answered a question. Quite often people who've been used to formal teaching in their own countries are very surprised by my methods. I know I shock some of them and they ask for books and grammar, but I concentrate

on making learning enjoyable with quizzes and games. I aim to make sure everyone has a laugh and that no one sits quietly but also that they all make great efforts to speak to me and to each other. I hope to send them out of my first class buzzing with excitement. After a couple of classes, people frequently bring friends, neighbours and other members of their family to join the class.

Achievement

The first session should not be all jollity and nothing else. By the time the session ends, everyone should have achieved at least one piece of relevant learning. There are various reasons why this is desirable:

- people have joined to *learn* – if they only wanted social contact they would have chosen a purely social event;
- it helps to get them over the hump of anxiety;
- it gives them a fair taste of what is to come;
- it reinforces motivation.

These first tasks need only be small. At the same time they should be challenging and carefully designed to make sure that everyone can get them right. When carried out successfully, such tactics can have powerfully energizing effects, as this trainee television studio director reports:

> At the very first session we all had a go at directing a simple sequence of changing captions to music – 'A, you're adorable; B, you're so beautiful . . .' etc. Looking back it was exquisitely simple. At the time it was terrifying, but fun and achievable. Everyone had a go and more or less everyone went away on a high. We'd sat in the hot seat and got pictures on the screen!

The combination of fun, challenge and group support can mean that people achieve what seemed previously like impossible feats. Here is an account of a beginners' swimming lesson which did just that:

In the first ten minutes every single one of us took our feet off the bottom. Okay, it was using a float, a rope or armbands, it wasn't real swimming, but considering that we were all non-swimmers and that several of us had serious doubts about our ability ever to swim it was amazing. Personally I was busting with pride that I'd got over a lifetime's fear. The boost to my morale was so tremendous that I actually swam a few strokes unaided during the second lesson and swam a whole width during the third.

These first tasks must be true to the focus of the rest of the course. Don't introduce bogus exercises which will make learners feel patronized later. Keep the methods of the first session consistent with whatever you plan for later. Don't, for instance make this mistake:

> She kept telling us that the course was all about participation and that our contributions would be a valuable part of the learning. The trouble was that the whole of the first day was taken up with lectures. There was no participation to be seen anywhere.

This kind of difficulty can happen because participants are thought to need a dose of 'orientation' before the 'real' work of the course begins. If this tends to happen on your courses, ask yourself whether it is essential for it to happen face to face. Might the same 'orientation' be achieved more easily and less obtrusively by giving people a paper to read, an exercise to do or a video to watch in advance of that first meeting?

Start and finish on time

Be wary of waiting for latecomers, however tempting it may seem. The people who have arrived on time will feel let down. Soon everyone will start coming late because 'the class never starts on time'. If you start late but finish on time, you may look as if you are cheating students out of their due. If you 'make up for it' by finishing late, then your final few minutes are likely to be disrupted by people creeping out. Begin and end as you mean to go on: promptly.

After the first session

Evaluate

Always ask yourself how it has gone and how it could have gone better. Ask the participants for feedback, and if you are working with a colleague, sit down and assess the event together. Evaluation is a big topic (see Chapter 11) and it's especially important to review and evaluate the first session.

Lecturing and demonstrating sometimes appeal to organizers on the grounds that they are 'economical' ways of using a tutor's time: they do not involve elaborate technician or administrative support. However, no teaching method can be described as economical if it fails to meet the prime objective of helping students learn.

Some tutors, of course, are drawn to teaching simply because they are good at talking, and enjoy it. Even teachers who are initially shy of their class may discover to their own amazement that the chance to talk uninterruptedly goes to their heads:

> It's like a drug once you've got a bit of confidence. You see the class sitting there and they're all listening to you! It's terribly flattering! You begin to think you're wonderfully eloquent and clever. It's only if and when the numbers drop off that you wonder whether you have quite the gifts of rhetoric that you hoped.

Earlier chapters have drawn attention to some of the major disadvantages of methods like lecturing and demonstrating, but it is worth reiterating them here, too. They are a strain on the already weak short-term memory capacity of adults. They proceed at one pace, which is most unlikely to suit even a majority of the class. Adults learn best through participation and activity, both of which are absent from straight lectures and demonstrations. Research has also consistently shown that lectures are a poor method of changing attitudes. In one classic experiment in the 1940s, Kurt Lewin compared the effectiveness of discussion and lectures in persuading housewives to try serving whale meat. Thirty-two per cent of the discussion group members claimed later they had actually served whale meat, compared with a minute 3 per cent from the group which had received a lecture.

Feedback is difficult, too. Once launched on what to you is an enjoyable exposition of your subject, it is easy for you to be blind to boredom, restlessness or incomprehension in your class. Adults are, in any case, often diffident about admitting there is a process or idea they have not understood. Conventional teaching techniques like lecturing and demonstration frequently help teacher and learner conspire together to cover up failure:

The do-it-yourself class was taken by a retired local builder. I remember the time we 'learnt' plastering. He'd just go sweeping up the wall – 'Whoosh!' lovely. He talked all the time, but we were never told how to go 'whoosh' ourselves. However, he did pause for a few seconds from time to time to say 'Any questions?' There never were any. To answer our questions he'd have needed to go right back to minus square one and he made you feel he was going to get through his syllabus or bust, so we let him get on with it, nodding all the while as if we did understand. It was less trouble to leave the class than to explain to him that he was going about 50 times too fast.

Even the claim that lectures can be 'inspirational' may be more pious hope than reality. Most of us have sat through innumerable lectures of one sort or another, but how many are truly memorable in retrospect? Most tutors are simply incapable of routinely supplying the acting ability, originality and panache which an 'inspirational' lecture requires.

In spite of all these disadvantages, both lecturing and demonstrating have their place in the range of techniques suitable for adults. Lecturing may be a poor way of stimulating thought or changing attitudes, but research has consistently shown that it is at least as good as (though not better than) most other methods at teaching information.

Lecturing seems to be an excellent way of supplying the framework of a subject into which students can slot more learning as they acquire it through other methods. Demonstration also has advantages. It shows what a skilled performance looks like and provides a trail of visual clues which are much easier for students to remember than words alone.

However, you need to employ both methods thoughtfully. As with every type of teaching technique, they should never be the sole methods used and you can improve their effectiveness immensely by careful preparation and presentation.

First, it is best to keep them short. Fifteen or twenty minutes of an uninterrupted 'performance' is as much as most adults can absorb. The limit for demonstrations probably ought to be even shorter – five minutes.

The importance of stories

Human beings love narrative. Dry facts do not engage people's attention. Always work out how you can tell a story instead of reciting facts or giving opinions.

Learn from journalism: human interest is what keeps people's attention. Even if the points you want to make are dry facts, think carefully about how to make them come alive through human interest. Some ways of doing this are to:

- make it personal;
- describe your own story as you struggled to understand/come to terms with whatever your theme is;
- tell other people's stories;
- describe the human conflict that your topic creates – e.g. any associated moral dilemmas.

It will help if you keep scrupulously to the main points. The intricate examples, meandering anecdotes and funny stories which may enliven a printed page are usually simply a distraction from the meaning of a verbally delivered piece, where the audience is committed to the speaker's pace.

Conveying confidence and authority

However wonderful your content, you will impress even more if you convey confidence and authority. We remember *how* someone has talked long after we have forgotten most of the content.

Using your body

Always stand – you cannot convey authority if you are sitting down. Stand with your body in a straight but not rigid line facing your audience straight on. Beware of:

- leaning on one foot;
- crossing one leg over the other;
- cocking your head to one side like a bird listening for worms;

- hopping;
- turning slightly away from the audience with one shoulder.

All of these convey lack of authority.

Keep your shoulders down – this conveys relaxation. Keep your hands lightly together or straight at your sides with the fingers pointing loosely down. Don't do a fig-leaf (hands over your genital area) or 'pious preacher' (hands 'steepled'). Use your notes judiciously – try not to get fixated by them; *never* use them as a barrier to hide behind. Mentally stake out your space and use it to take a few steps backwards and forwards while you are speaking. If you remain rooted to the spot you will convey 'tethered elephant' and if you pace about too much, 'caged lion' – neither is desirable.

Mannerisms

Ask someone you trust to give you feedback about any mannerisms you might have which could distract while giving your lecture or demonstration. They all come from nervousness and you may not be aware of them. Common ones include:

- nervous little coughs;
- jingling change or keys in your pocket;
- scratching;
- pushing glasses up your nose;
- pushing or tossing hair away from your face;
- frowning.

Your voice

Check that everyone can hear you before you get going properly and pause for two or three seconds before starting your presentation – this gives a little added drama and allows you to get your thoughts together. Remember to use pauses to add impact and use the whole of your mouth to speak. If you know you have difficulties with volume, it may help to practise projecting your voice.

Keeping in touch with the group

It can feel scary to be the focus of all those eyes, but with practice you will feel more comfortable. This alarm is often well justified. The longer you continue your solo performance, the more opportunity you are giving the group for critical appraisal of your mannerisms, dress and voice:

> It's almost like coming into a room naked. You know they can see every tremor in your hands, hear every shake in your voice, observe every change of colour, notice only too well when you're not completely master of your material. After all, what else have they got to look at?

> It was his voice that got me in the end . . . it just ground on and on. And he always had stains on his tie!

One of the best ways to keep people's attention is to use the *lighthouse effect* – raking your audience slowly from one side to the other throughout your presentation. This means that you are engaging everyone in a few seconds of regular eye contact. It retains their interest and creates the impression that you are talking to each person individually. It also gives you immediate feedback – who is looking bored, asleep, fidgety?

Beware of talking to:

- only one side of the room;
- the ceiling;
- your notes;
- your graphics;
- the flipchart;
- your feet;
- one or two smiley people in the audience;
- the tops of the chairs;
- the spaces between people's chairs.

The other important rule to remember is to *smile*. If you look too serious people will lose interest. Show passion and enthusiasm. If you are not enthusiastic about your subject why should anyone else be?

Handouts

You can reduce some of the disadvantages of the lecture or demonstration by making sure that people have handouts. There are some simple, common-sense rules which will help make your handouts as useful as possible. First, don't attempt to give people every word you intend to say: no one will read anything lengthy. Try to limit handout material to no more than two pages of well laid out text. Restrict yourself to your main points. Write clearly and unambiguously – ask yourself whether the handout will make sense to someone who has not been present at your session. If not, think again, it probably lacks clarity.

People are surrounded by excellence in graphic design all day every day, so a sloppily prepared sheet will convey a poor impression. If you are using colour, stick to no more than three. Keep the pages uncluttered with cross-headings and a reasonable type size – nothing smaller than 12 point. Keep the page uncluttered and also keep to lower case type – all capitals makes for a hard read. Look at any motorway sign for a good example of clever use of lower case letters easily read at a glance even by a speeding motorist. If you are using diagrams, keep the lettering horizontal – it's not pleasant to have to turn a page upside down in order to read the labels. Where you have to present figures, use bar or pie charts – they are much easier to read. Finally, avoid clipart drawings because everyone has seen them hundreds of times and they are clichéd.

If you are using PowerPoint for your presentation, you can produce a small-scale version of each slide without having to waste huge quantities of paper on photocopying.

Always give people any printed material *after* you have spoken, unless there is a case for offering them the chance to make notes while you speak.

Notes

With experience you will be able to give a lecture or presentation without any notes – the best option of all because you can

Table 6.1 Making and using notes

Writing out in full.	Reassuring, but stultifying – it always sounds as if you are reading and you have to keep your eyes down, thus losing contact with your audience.
Writing out a précis of the full version.	Better, but A4 sheets can be bulky.
Reducing the content to cards with key words only. *Tip*: punch a hole in the corner and put a treasury tag or ring through them so that they cannot get out of order even if you drop them.	Best if you need notes. Cards are easily handled and make a smaller barrier than sheets of paper.
Using an overhead projector. *Tip 1*: don't overdo it – the audience will keep looking at the screen and not at you. Restrict yourself to no more than seven slides in a 20-minute presentation and turn the projector off between slides to reduce noise and distraction. *Tip 2*: add Post-its to the slides to remind you of any key points.	Useful if you can remember not to keep looking behind you at the screen. Gives the group something else to look at.
Using PowerPoint	Looks professional but has disadvantages, as above. Check that the venue can cope with the technology.
Using flipcharts prepared in advance. *Tip*: resist the temptation to keep turning to the flipchart and talking to it rather than to the audience.	Looks informal and also gives the audience something to look at other than you.

engage fully with your group. If you are less experienced, you will need notes for the reassurance they give against 'drying' – usually the inexperienced tutor's ultimate nightmare. The various options for notes are shown in Table 6.1.

Handling questions

Occasionally you may need to give a formal lecture followed by questions from the audience at the end. It goes without saying that it is important to demonstrate respect for the questioner at all times. Keep eye contact throughout the entire question and answer sequence and listen to the complete question carefully. You can probably anticipate obvious questions and come prepared.

Keep your answers short – there will probably be others in the group who want to have their say. Conclude with 'Did I answer your question?' to make sure that the questioner is satisfied. Where you get challenging or apparently aggressive questions, beware of the trap of answering at the questioner's expense – you're not at the hustings or dealing with hecklers. Self-deprecating humour often works, so does stating the obvious – 'That's a difficult question'. Where you have a long-winded questioner, wait until they pause for breath and break in quickly with 'I believe I can answer that . . .'

Playing for time is often important. For instance, you may need a few seconds to make sure you've understood the question or to consider your answer. You can try any of these tactics:

- staying deliberately cool;
- repeating the question;
- asking the questioner to repeat the question;
- asking for clarification;
- asking the questioner to answer their own question – for instance, 'that's a good question. Before answering, I'd like to hear your answer'.

Sometimes a challenging question is actually a statement in disguise. The give-away here is 'Wouldn't you agree that . . .'.

There may be no need to reply at all, other than to say something like 'That's a very interesting contribution to the debate. Thanks for making that point'.

A note on demonstrations

A demonstration is a lecture with actions. The same basic principles apply as to lectures. You may need to think about whether you face the group or find some way for them to see the action from the operator's point of view. If you make no provision for this, your students will always have to reverse your hand movements, which is confusing to say the least. Cookery schools solve this problem with large mirrors. My dance teachers do it by having a radio mike and keeping their backs to the group so that their right or left legs and ours are facing the same way.

I learnt a lot about demonstrations from shooting cookery programmes for television. It was always vital to have everything the presenter needed laid out as if for a medical operation. This meant that utensils, ingredients etc. were set out in the order that they would be used and all containers were made of transparent materials as far as possible, to increase the chances that all the details would be easy to see even on a poor-quality home monitor. No one ever wants to see an onion being chopped every time a recipe included one, so these and other ingredients would be pre-prepared. The principles apply to anything where there is a natural sequence to the demonstration. If it's a complicated one, have a dry run at home – this will usually reveal what you have forgotten.

The core dangers with demonstrations are over-simplifying and going too fast. As an expert, you will probably have forgotten what it feels like (if you ever knew) to be a complete beginner or to have little natural aptitude for a skill. It is all too easy to make unwarranted assumptions about what people already know, to go too fast and, sadly, it must be said, to see the demo as a place where you show off. If you know this applies to you, slow down and check your assumptions with your group. Aim to give a few minutes of demo followed immediately by opportunities for the group to practise the sequence. A demonstration is not a *performance*, it's a way of showing what a skilled performance looks like when broken down into learnable bits – a very different emphasis.

As with every other type of teaching method, you need to arrange the lecture or demonstration room and its furniture carefully in advance. Spare chairs are best removed altogether. Curved rows will give a greater feeling of 'belonging' and therefore more chance of participation than straight ones. A hollow square round a table will encourage more questioning than rows. A large room provides bad acoustics for a quiet voice and encourages the development of vast spaces between students. Students who need to take notes need a firm surface to rest on.

In general, lectures and demonstrations are probably best used in short bursts, with frequent recourse to alternative methods of learning like discussion, individual practice, projects or reading. Far too many lecturers and demonstrators assume that their listeners have some hole in the head into which information can conveniently be poured. As Thomas Carlyle wisely said, 'Too much faith is commonly placed in oral lessons and lectures. To be poured into like a bucket is not exhilarating to any soul.'

Chapter 7

▶ Case studies, role-play, simulation and games

Guests wandering through the hotel could be forgiven for their amazement. There, apparently furiously engaged, are three small groups of senior managers making and flying paper planes. Standing over them is someone with a stopwatch, a ruler and a stern expression. The feverish activity continues until the hotel lobby is covered with discarded planes. One group looks distinctly cross – they are obviously not doing so well. One group looks pleased with itself, the other moderately so. What is going on? The explanation is *management development*, but it will not be immediately apparent to a casual observer. If this is a public sector organization should someone write a furious letter to *The Times* denouncing the whole thing as a scandalous waste of money?

Well, no. These managers are engaged in a powerful simulation, and are discovering at first hand what it takes to lead a team through engaging in a competitive exercise. Unknown to them, the three groups are being led in different ways and the participants are finding out in the most vivid and direct way possible what makes for effective team leadership. What the casual observer will not see is the two-hour long debrief where the theoretical construct is explained and people's experience looked at in a calmer light than the feverish excitement of the simulation itself.

This will include helping the losing group to understand that the reason they did not do well in the exercise was because of the nature of the leadership they received. Many of this group are likely to be feeling angry – with each other, with the trainer and with the exercise. They will need skilled help in understanding that this is all part of the learning. This group has been taking part in a *simulation* which might also be described as a *game*.

In the totally different environment of a reconfigured church, something apparently very different is going on. Here, volunteers for a self-help charity are receiving training in how to deal with distressed and incoherent telephone callers. In the former vestry, the trainer miraculously turns herself into a variety of 'callers' while the trainee volunteer helper tries to deal with the 'call', watched by the five other members of the group. After the call is over, the group will debrief on what happened and will unpick the learning. If the trainee has not done particularly well, the trainer may rerun the activity so that the participant can learn from the feedback he or she has received. This is classic *role-play*.

Meanwhile, in what appears to be a very different course and setting, a group of very young doctors are practising their emergency life-saving techniques – cardio-pulmonary resuscitation (CPR). You cannot practise CPR properly on a living person. So these doctors are learning through a clever dummy called 'Annie' which will tell them through a printout and with great accuracy how effective their mouth-to-mouth breathing has been and whether they have been compressing the chest in the right place and with the right degree of pressure. This is *simulation*.

More conventionally, a group of young managers is learning how to make robust selection decisions. Each has a pack of materials – application forms, a set of criteria for a job and a folio of other documents. They have to decide which candidates they would shortlist on the basis of what they have in front of them. Elsewhere in the same training centre, another group is looking at a reprinted article from the *Harvard Business Review* which sets out a fictional account of one manager's difficulties. The group will discuss the case and will put forward suggestions about what they would do if they had been in the same situation. Both these approaches are *case study*.

In all these groups the tutor has found a solution through the various techniques to the problem of how to involve adult students in the acquistition of an apparently intractable and complex mass of knowledge. The easy, neat method in every case would have been to deliver a lecture. The 'rules' of effective leadership could be explained along with the various theories behind them. The essentials of how to counsel distressed people could be explained by describing them, as could some simple guidelines on how to shortlist candidates for a job. The young doctors could pick up any first-aid book for a clear account of how to give CPR. However, none of these approaches on their own would be likely to be as effective as the alternatives I have described here. Simulation, role-play, case study and games are not universal panaceas, but they are exceptionally powerful techniques. I use them constantly in the training I run myself.

When to choose these techniques

I use simple criteria:

- Does this event need to include something pacey, involving and fun?
- Is there a principle here that has to be experienced to be fully understood?
- Where there is a skill involved:
  - is it unlikely that people will have a realistic view of how skilful they actually are?
  - can the skill be improved with feedback?
  - is it difficult to practise the skill easily or safely in the 'real world'?

Where you answer any of these questions with 'yes', then there is a case for using the techniques described in this chapter.

There is nothing especially difficult or even novel about using simulations and care studies. Simulation as a way of learning has a long history because it is so obviously useful, but in modern times it was pioneered by the British and US armies during World War II and has continued to be an important part of military training. Most TV documentaries are case studies and role-play has become increasingly common in management development courses. Many classic board games are also simulations in their way – for instance, Monopoly and chess.

The simplest way of understanding the four techniques is to look at them as four increasingly elaborate and participatory versions of the same basic art – a way of learning general principles through being involved in a particular situation, usually one which could occur in real life, but with some of the real-life time intervals and distracting detail smoothed out for purposes of laying bare the essentials.

Case studies can be prepared through folders of documents, collections of descriptive material, tapes, video or a mixture of all these, and would be presented to a group simply as the basis of discussion. Role-playing takes the process a stage further, when members of the group act out and improvise roles and situations using the information they obtained from the case-study material. This might become a full-scale simulation if it were carried out continuously and intensively over several hours using fairly elaborate printed or recorded material, with fresh problems and complications introduced from time to time by the tutor. A simulation becomes a game at the point where it turns into a competition between individuals or groups with points awarded for completing a task, usually under time pressure.

How is this type of exercise organized and carried out? Some role-playing is so simple that it hardly needs any preparation at all and is absorbed without fuss into work already being done. For instance, in a discussion on running meetings, it would be perfectly natural for a tutor to suggest that instead of simply talking about different kinds of chairing, the students might actually try them. In language teaching, role-playing may seem a normal extension of work done practising dialogues and drills, and only becomes more recognizably something novel and different when the tutor sets up a 'scene' with the appropriate props.

For instance, in one French conversation class the tutor bases the first part of the class time on an episode from a broadcast language series where the characters are ordering food in a restaurant. The students sit in their normal places while they are repeating the dialogue and drills, but they then move in groups of four to a table in one corner of the room which is perfectly laid out for a meal. The tablecloth, wine, knives and forks, butter, mustard, menu, bread-basket and, finally, money are all French. The students 'play' the characters in the series, but extend the dialogue according to improvisations of their own and in response to the tutor, who sometimes plays waiter, sometimes another diner. After corrections and discussion they then play the same scene again.

Some tutors prefer to involve members of the group in researching the case-study material themselves: preparing speeches for a debate, or preparing a case for negotiation in an industrial agreement is one way of doing this. In this case the tutor simply presents the group with the barest outlines of the situation a week or a few days beforehand. Others favour variations on what is known in management training as an 'in-tray exercise', where the group members are presented with a batch of case-study material – letters, records, memos, press reports – such as might appear in an in-tray, and are required as individuals and under considerable time pressure to reach the kinds of decision they may need to make in real life.

More usually, tutors will involve the whole class in group activity, either all together, in small groups, or in small groups which watch each other and then discuss. Sometimes they will deliberately hold back certain crucial pieces of information and will wait for the group to ask for it; sometimes they will supply a group or an individual with background information or documents not available to the others.

Here is an example, taken from a full-scale simulation designed to suit a three-hour session planned for a group of parents on 'Education Today'. The simulation centres on a case study (details disguised but taken from a real-life case) of an 11-year-old whose parents were faced with the tricky problem of wanting their child to go to a different school from the one in which she was offered a place by the education authority. The aims of the simulation were: to inform parents about the current system in their area; to explain their legal rights within it; to explore some of the personal stresses involved in parent–school relationships; and to discuss the criteria on which choice of school might be based.

The documents themselves would be too lengthy to reproduce here but they included:

1 The child's last primary-school report.
2 A medical report.
3 Two essays written by the child on 'My Ideal School' and 'My Family'.
4 Confidential report on the child from the primary-school head to the chief education officer.
5 Copies of correspondence between parents, heads and the chief education officer.
6 Long extracts from the two secondary-school prospectuses.
7 Extracts from relevant Education Acts.
8 Extracts from 'Manual of Guidance' for parents.

Advantages

When done well, what are the advantages of this type of learning? First, the element of realism makes it an eminently suitable way for adults to learn. Adults are impatient of teaching which seems remote from the realities of whichever skill they are learning; we want to feel that no time is wasted on vague theory which is going to be of little real relevance and practical value. Thus, if a course for managers is called 'Managing Discipline' the course members may not take at all kindly to lectures on economic or historic theory, however vital the lecturer might feel this information is to understanding current conflicts. Members of such courses are inclined to say that since they conduct their real-life negotiations in an atmosphere of hustling, keen controversy, they expect to see the same atmosphere understood and catered for on the course. It is even better if the same realistic conditions can enter the process of learning itself, only in a way that more information can be fed in, in conditions of more certain control than is usual in real life, where inflamed or tender feelings can mean a stubborn refusal to accept new information at all. The realistic atmosphere in simulation is achieved through the careful preparation of the stimulus material, and also by the fact that students take roles where they start behaving as people might in a wider variety of situations than is possible in real life.

Simulation can also bring an element of realism and excitement to academic subjects by inviting decisions in a re-created historical, geographical or sociological situation. Thus students of history who might be studying the Battle of Waterloo could be given maps of the battleground, pins to represent groups of soldiers in the different armies, letters, memoranda, biographies, and so on, and could play out for themselves the crucial moves of the battle. In teaching geography to children, some successful games have been developed around events such as the building of the great North American railways, where children have in fact learnt the geography of the country, the map of the routes, and the reasons railways were built when and where they were through the use of a geography game. No doubt simulations could be developed along the same line for adults.

A second important advantage of role-playing and simulation is that they are entirely active methods of learning. In earlier chapters I have tried to show how important activity is to adult learning, and have stressed how adults need to avoid being 'told' how to do something, but need instead to try it out for themselves. Indeed, simulation may offer a unique chance in certain subjects to bridge the gap between theory and practice. This can be one of the most unyielding problems of planning a piece of teaching where, as in management or teacher training, students will frequently complain that the theory they learnt was a hopelessly inadequate preparation for facing real life. Some kind of simulation or role-play may be the most effective way that managers can learn how to conduct an interview or chair a meeting. It is also an excellent way of generating a variety of solutions to problems – for instance, complex interpersonal situations where there is rarely one 'right' answer.

A further advantage of simulation and role-play here is that because it is a realistic, active method, it has many of the features of learning in real life, with the powerful difference that in real life mistakes made can be expensive, disagreeable and mortifying. In role-play mistakes can be made without retribution.

The atmosphere of calm analysis and good-humoured support from tutor and other students makes it possible to see why mistakes have been made and to learn to avoid them in future. In this way a student, who in a business game makes a gross error which in real life would have cost her her job, can step back and analyse what moves led her (or the character she was playing) to act as she did. An added convenience is that because of its telescoped timescale, simulation can present students with situations they are unlikely to encounter every day, and might indeed wish to avoid, but which nevertheless they ought to be prepared to meet. Thus role-play and simulation in a public-speaking class might introduce a particularly odious heckler character; a management course for senior nurses might include a difficult situation both with clinical and managerial colleagues.

In a full-scale simulation this telescoped timescale has the further advantage that it makes it possible to see the effect of your decisions and actions in a rapid way that is not normally possible in real life – in other words, there is almost instant feedback.

Because role-playing usually arouses powerful emotions in those who take part, it can be a potent and valuable method to any tutor whose subject involves the development of sensitivity and tolerance. Crude attitude-change is not generally held to be a desirable educational aim in education, but increasing understanding in a way that may lead to attitude-change certainly is. In subjects such as politics, sociology, industrial relations, religion or literature, many issues can only be approached through a genuine understanding not just of one other point of view, but of the possibility that a whole range of viewpoints may be equally valid. Thus managers, often reluctantly persuaded at first to prepare a set of union as well as management cases for a piece of role-playing, may come to understand the strengths and weaknesses, the varying opinions at different levels of seniority, of both management and union in a way that would be impossible from a more passive, intellectualized analysis. Where 'role reversal' is used (after the first run-through, the participants play each other's roles), this effect is particularly noticeable.

Another benefit of this kind of role-playing and simulation is that their real value is often in the 'social skills' they teach. Supporters of this point of view would say that what is important on many courses is not so much absorbing the content of any particular mass of information as learning to understand how one's own behaviour appears to other people, to work in a group and to solve a problem, to accept other people's solutions, their contributions and their right to disagree. Where 'how' something is said is more important than 'what' is said, role-play may, indeed, be the only way of learning.

Specific aims

Most people enjoy role-playing and simulation. But the benefits are far from being confined to the emotional delights of acting out and creating conflict, discussion and debate. Role-playing and simulation can be designed specifically to meet some of the fundamentally serious aims of any course – to teach people how to acquire, evaluate and use information.

For example, a group who had enrolled for a course in urban planning undertook a simulation which was worked in pairs over two intensive four-hour sessions separated by a week. To work out several possible solutions to a single problem in traffic control and urban redevelopment, participants were obliged to look up, absorb and use some or all of: Town and Country Planning Acts; several classic studies in urban sociology; local history; academic analyses and appreciations of Georgian architecture; and some elementary principles of civil engineering. During the course of the simulation their tutor presented them with additional complications in the form of resolutions passed by a local pressure group, or announcements of new findings on sites of historical value. Here, the group was involved in a highly sophisticated and elaborate project involving research skills, information retrieval and problem solving, as well as learning to weigh social priorities and to argue and present a case in a final report. The students' own opinion of the exercise was, devastatingly, that they had learnt more in the two simulation classes and in the following class devoted to discussion and analysis than they had learnt in all the rest of the course put together.

Involvement

There seems no doubt that simulation and role-playing generate intense involvement among those taking part and that they are an excellent way of motivating people who might find it difficult to learn in other ways. It is almost impossible to remain aloof and uninvolved. Even the most stately student usually finds it hard to stay outside. Most students start by thinking it is going to be a laugh, something they will go along with to humour their tutor. They then rapidly pass to the stage where they are involved but keep some superficial sense of joking distance or irony. In a class such as the urban planning group where the basic emphasis is on academic skills this often remains the predominant mood. Where the whole group is also involved in role-playing, even this mood passes, replaced by an entirely absorbed seriousness for the task in hand.

Simulation and role-playing are immensely adaptable for classes of mixed ability. They can offer natural opportunities for working in groups, for occasions where students of different abilities can help each other, and where distinctions between the bright and not so bright can at least be blurred if not extinguished altogether.

The tutor's role

Many tutors are bothered by the apparent inevitability of their own dominance in the classroom. Simulation involves a fundamental change in your role. You are still very much in the centre of things since you prepare at least the initial materials, and in the class you will usually retain a central and coordinating position. Nevertheless, your most hectic work is done before the class meets, and your traditional role of giving information to all your students simultaneously is certainly eroded. The emphasis shifts to the resources used, to the students themselves, and to the creative contributions they are able to make with your encouragement. In this way, too, the 'problem' of student participation melts away. Students participate as a matter of course because activity is built into the whole exercise.

Problems of resources

Every novelty in educational method brings with it some danger that devotees will recommend it as a cure-all for every classroom malaise. It is unlikely that any one method will be right for every class, and this is as true of simulation, case studies and role-play as of any other method. Role-playing and simulation are not all plain sailing for teacher or learner. Although they are highly flexible methods and, once prepared, can be used with a variety of different classes, the preparation can be lengthy and exacting.

Emotional display

Tutors who have not used role-playing and simulation tend to brood anxiously about the potential dangers of inviting too much emotional involvement from students. Adult classrooms generally tend to be peaceful places and you may hesitate before plunging your students into what might turn out to be an embarrassing emotional display.

It is for this reason, no doubt, that, of the techniques described in this chapter, case study is by far the most commonly used, precisely because it allows emotional issues germane to the group to be discussed coolly at a distance in terms of other people's problems, but without any of the apparent hazards involved in role-playing. It is true that in role-playing some students may be alarmed by the passionate response a role-play draws from them or from others. It is true that some role-playing becomes nearly indistinguishable from the real thing. But in practice it is never quite the real thing, tempers never run quite so high, your emotions are never quite so fully engaged as they are in the real situation, because, however realistic the setting, the problem, or the incidental detail, you never forget that you are in a classroom. Particularly where the tutor has stressed that it is not their own but other people's roles that students are to play, there is always some sense of distance between action and thought. In a group which has become experienced in using the technique, there is a noticeable feeling that it is quite all right to indulge the emotions a situation may provoke because these emotions are in themselves valuable source material for the follow-up discussion and analysis.

Student anxieties

A more real difficulty, especially at first, is the opposite one that adult students may refuse to become involved at all, they may not wish to step out of the conventionally passive student role into something that seems to bear a suspicious resemblance to amateur dramatics. A student who is nervous about speaking in public may be even more embarrassed about role-playing. This difficulty arises most often where role-playing is used in academic subjects, when it will be most noticeably in conflict with traditional methods of teaching and where it probably grows less naturally and genuinely out of the work than out of subjects where the basic art being taught is skill in human relationships. A student who has enrolled for what looks like being a straightforward enough course in international relations may well feel as peeved about the introduction of academic gaming as the customer who finds that a comfortable, undemanding local pub has gone in for poetry readings. If role-playing and simulation can only be introduced with a great fanfare and with much special pleading from you, then they are probably unsuited to the course. In any case, they are probably best tried gradually, without fuss and on a small scale at first.

Problems for the tutor

One of the reasons students may be suspicious of role-playing and simulation is that they are not orderly, predictable methods of learning. There are no prepackaged maxims that can be transferred direct from tutor to learner. On the contrary, students not only have to elaborate on a given situation by actively interpreting it, they then have to deduce the general rules for themselves. This is why the follow-up discussion is so important. It is also why learning through simulation, role-playing and case study takes so much longer and is so much more diffuse and sprawling than a series of lectures. Use of these techniques, therefore, makes considerable demands on the tutor, not only in the time and skill they will demand in preparation, but also in your ability to train your groups to generalize a clear overall picture from a series of specific examples.

Perhaps the most common practical difficulty is that tutors are often unable to encourage the group to look beyond the rights and wrongs of a particular case. If the material is sufficiently intriguing, group members will sometimes argue it endlessly, but take it no further than that. If the material is less absorbing, they may tend to discuss it in a desultory way for a short time, but will then dismiss it by implying that because conditions in their job, school or locality are not exactly like the ones in the case study, there is nothing to be learnt from it. This can be a particularly pressing problem with people who have a narrow but extremely intensive practical knowledge of their own cases while rejecting the applicability of either general theory or other cases to their own.

A first necessary step might be for you to demonstrate through role-play that even their own case looks different when seen from different angles, but progress here is bound to be slow. With such groups, case study, role-play and simulation done badly is particularly frustrating for the students, who are understandably inclined in such circumstances to start muttering in favour of bringing back formal methods where at least the outward trappings of learning are familiar.

Another real enough shortcoming, particularly of case-study techniques, is that there is never as much information available as there would be in real life. People will often criticize a slackly prepared case study on these grounds by saying that they cannot possibly argue the case without more information. I once sat in with a group of senior managers who were being invited to solve a problem based on a difficult business situation. Discussion was slow because the study itself had been too crudely drawn. In the end the group decided that the only way their discussion could be turned into something useful to themselves was for them to decide what extra information they would have needed in order to solve the problem. In real life there are, of course, often severe limitations to the amount of information that is available. Most tutors believe that case studies must and should omit confusing and conflicting detail, though some exponents of case-study and simulation techniques would stress that it is sometimes necessary to introduce this, too, to teach relevance and choice. But in general there must be simplification, not so much that the case is hopelessly falsified to the state where students will reject it, and never so complicated that it is beyond the current capacities of the group to solve. Where the case study is extended into role-play some of this danger recedes because the case itself takes on the added dimensions which active participation must give.

Making role-play work

In spite of all these problems, role-play in particular is a uniquely valuable technique – superb at helping people learn behavioural skills. It is probably the only way, for instance, that you could train adequately as a Samaritan, because it is the only technique that could give you supervised practice before you are let loose in the real world, where an untrained Befriender would quickly feel confused and inadequate as well as being potentially quite likely to behave unhelpfully with clients. It is certainly the best way for shop assistants to learn how to deal with customers. A few stints of role-played practice at handling an aggressive customer are worth any amount of written advice in the staff manual. But, like any other technique, role-play needs care in execution. Normally, you will need to work through all the following stages:

Objectives

Be clear about which objectives you are hoping to meet through role-play. Write yourself a tightly defined brief before you begin. For instance, if you are thinking of running a role-play on selection interviewing, it will probably not be helpful to think vaguely: 'Well, it will do them good to see it from the other person's point of view'. It will be better to write down something like: 'Having completed the role-play, the participants should be able to list ten examples of open-ended questions, describe 'hostile' body language, and so on.

Choose or design appropriate material

To work with your group, the material must be relevant, brief and credible. If you are writing your own, then you may need to check it out with a suitable 'reader' first: one tiny error (for instance, a wrong job title) could destroy the 'willing suspension of disbelief' in your group as surely as it does to spot a continuity error in a film. It is always better to base a role-play on a real situation if possible: this gives you the perfect reply to students who protest that such a scenario could 'never' happen, and is also likely to provide you with the small details and complexities that bring a case to life. But beware of 'scripting' a role-play too lengthily or in a way that leaves little room for manoeuvre and elaboration. People may feel constrained by all the detail or simply refuse to take part: 'I'm just not like that person, I wouldn't behave like that.'

Introduce and explain the benefits of role-play to the group

Role-play may be new to many of your group and they will need time to consider its virtues and drawbacks. If you intend to use the technique then you will need to sell its benefits vigorously. Explain the difference between 'role-play' and 'acting', and describe the normal progress of a typical role-play. It usually helps to quote the comments of former students who may themselves have been dubious about it at the start but who ended up convinced of its merits.

Give a detailed briefing before you begin

The briefing is part of the learning because here you introduce the ideas the role-play is designed to explore. Tell the group what your objectives are, what the 'rules' are about how much time is allowed, whether or not the players should confer in advance or consult you. This is also the stage to brief group members who are not 'playing' but observing. They could, for instance, have an 'observation sheet' which they fill in as the role-play progresses. If they are to observe an 'annual assessment' between a 'manager' and a 'subordinate', then they could have a sheet which lists different behaviours which they tick or cross. Tell the observers what you expect them to do later – normally to give feedback to the players. Depending on the type of role-play, you may like to give different observers different types of task – for instance one set could observe the 'manager' and one the 'subordinate'.

Run the role-play

Keeping it brief has the virtue that several 'players' (say three pairs) can take part. Five minutes of role-play will often generate twice as much discussion. Be prepared to step in if the role-play wilts or becomes too intense or begins to ramble away from the main issue.

Debriefing

There is no point in role-play without debriefing. It is the process of debriefing which helps make the learning points. It is often wise to let the role-players have the first word. 'How did you think that went?' 'What did you think of the way you handled X?' 'How did it compare with the way you deal with this in real life?' Giving the role-players this first chance to speak allows them to wind down and step back from the role. It also establishes a helpfully self-critical atmosphere.

Next, ask the observers for their feedback. You will already have established the same rules for sensitive and helpful feedback as you use yourself (see Chapter 2 for detailed hints on how to do this) but this process must be handled with infinite care, especially when people have been playing a role which is near to their own real circumstances and where it is reasonable to assume that they will therefore be extra-vulnerable to clumsily-offered negative feedback.

Now make the transition into a general discussion about underlying themes. These can be prepared in advance. Has the role-play thrown up general trends or difficulties which parallel problems in the real world? Has it revealed insights (we hope that it has) into how similar issues may be handled 'for real'? What tends to get in the way of the 'ideal' solution?

Finally, don't forget to thank and praise the players for their efforts. This is important: many people will have taken part vigorously, but may privately wonder later if they have lost face by doing so. Forestall this reaction by making it clear that it is entirely thanks to their skill and commitment that such a valuable discussion was possible.

Refine the role-play

Running a role-play for the first time will usually reveal some flaws in its design. Regard the first run as a pilot; make suitable alterations in the light of useful comments from students or observations of your own.

Chapter **8**

▶ Discussion and facilitation

In the quotes below all the tutors and students quoted felt sure that 'discussion' accurately described what was going on in their courses:

> After an hour-and-a-quarter lecture from me we have a coffee break, then discussion. The class usually raises such pertinent points that lengthy answers are needed from me, so that it sometimes needs miniature lectures to give a satisfactory reply. The class is exhausting for this reason.

> During discussion we are speaking to each other, exploring, exchanging views, learning from each other: tutor from student, students from tutor, students from students.

> I dislike the discussion part of the class because some members (not me) always lose their tempers.

> He is a very good teacher and we have a lot of interesting discussions, but he does love us to come round to his point of view!

> In discussion I believe in quick-fire, question-and-answer technique. It keeps them on their toes.

> I encourage them to be frank. The content of the course (psychology) is less important than the business of learning to work as a group and getting to know yourself. I say virtually nothing. They do all the talking.

Clearly, there are wide variations in the activities of these courses. One tutor seems to talk all the time, another says 'virtually nothing'; the atmosphere of the discussion in one class is mild and conversational, in another it is fierce and argumentative, in yet another personal and intense. Most important of all, all the quotes show something of the fundamental divergencies of opinion about the purpose and value of the discussion process itself, a divergence often concealed by the umbrella of a word such as 'discussion' which has such vague and uncomfortable associations.

Some tutors clearly believe that the point of a discussion is to change the attitudes of the class, usually in the direction of the tutor's views on a particular issue. Others believe in discussion because students enjoy it and they think there should be parts of a class which students enjoy. Others again are never quite sure why they do it, but feel that somehow it must be a good thing. With this theoretical vagueness 'discussion', as it is usually applied, can mean anything from a few questions tossed to a class at the end of a gruelling lecture session to a solemn 90 minutes given over entirely to something very near group therapy.

What is 'discussion'?

Group therapy has its value, so does a question-and-answer session, so does a debate, but none of these processes is authentic discussion. A rough definition of real, as opposed to imitation, discussion might be that it is a situation where students and tutor can and do give an open, equal and personal response to a book, a philosophical theory, an industrial-relations problem, a current fashion in dress, a social trend, or anything else which needs interpretation to take it beyond a factual statement. The implications of this sort of discussion are that in controversial personal, social and academic areas, students, as adult members of society, have as much right to articulate and expect respect for their points of view as do tutors.

Discussion defined in this way is a very different thing from what passes for discussion in many adult classes. It becomes a time when tutors show their classes that they have abandoned their teaching roles as such, that they are encouraging what R.W.K. Paterson describes as a 'common search for meanings. For two people to "discuss" some piece of news is for them to ask each other "What does it mean?"'[1]

This search for meanings is frequently given the educational justification that it consolidates knowledge, improves the social atmosphere of the group, allows people to test themselves, and so on, but in fact discussion is in itself a supremely valuable process, whether it is used for a few minutes in a computing class or whether it becomes the main method of learning in a sociology group. To quote Paterson again:

> To unfold the meaning of a poem by discovering oneself and one's world in face of the poem, to experience the sympathetic, critical, understanding, puzzled, consenting, or demurring responses of others similarly occupied, and to respond in turn to their self-disclosures and self-commitments – to do all this is surely to engage in a type of activity which is educationally ultimate.

Facilitation

Perhaps the word *discussion* is now more clearly understood to be the process you use as a tutor when what you are doing is *facilitating*. Facilitation is a vital tool for anyone who is helping adults learn. Literally it means *to make easy*. It's vital whenever any of these conditions apply:

- *No one has all the power*. This is fundamentally true of most situations where adults are learning. Your group can abandon its learning at any point: they are not prisoners. Even if they do not physically walk out, they may subvert in thousands of ways. The only way to treat adults in a learning situation is as equals.
- *No one knows the answer*. There are few subjects where it is legitimate to insist on one opinion. Take any subject you like: the origins of the universe, whether last night's sitcom

136 *Adults learning*

was any good, whether the latest war is justified, how to cure
a cold, if or how developing countries ought to be helped,
whether women are better drivers than men, the best way to
deflea a cat . . . whatever the subject, it is likely that there will
be as many opinions as there are people.
- *It is important for people to own their opinions.* This is part of
  what makes for learning. The struggle to gather the facts, to
  weigh them up, to seek out your own emotional bias and
  prejudices, to come to conclusions to which you feel commitment, not compliance – this is what makes for excellence
  in learning.

Where it is important for your group to do these three things, then
you will need to facilitate and to do so by leading a discussion.

Facilitation is not the same as any of these activities, which
may look superficially similar:

- *Chairing a meeting* has an end point which usually results in
  agreeing a decision.
- *Chairing a debate* where the confrontational format is designed
  to emphasize differences in order to explore an issue.
- *Group therapy* where the point is cure. The aim is to do it
  through group exploration on the assumption that members
  of the group are dysfunctional. Members of learning groups
  may feel dysfunctional in other aspects of their lives at some
  point – who doesn't? But when your aim is learning pure and
  simple you must make the assumption that you are working
  with healthy, resourceful people. Group therapy leaders use
  facilitation skills, but the end purpose is different.

Tutors and authority

Many tutors would claim that they already have the sort of
respect for their students which makes the discussions in their
classrooms as free as it is possible to make them. However, we
can too easily assume the mantle of authority the profession
has acquired from teaching children. Furthermore, many of us
are unaware of how much influence we have with our classes

and of how easily this influence can be exerted affectionately as well as brusquely. It is often as easy for the teacher of adults to do this as it is for the schoolteacher, given the diffidence of an inexperienced adult student, or of a new class of learners anxious not to declare themselves too soon:

> I thought I'd let other people do all the talking. I felt too ignorant to open my mouth.

> I knew I'd blush if I spoke, so I never spoke.

> Discussion is all right for those who are well informed. Other people always seem to know so much more than me.

Classroom discussions, closely analysed, will often reveal how frequently tutors capitalize on their traditional authority and on the humble feelings of their students. As a result, many discussions in adult education and training are far from free or equal, because tutors, often quite unconsciously, guide, manipulate and dominate proceedings. For instance, you may feel obliged to follow every comment from a student with a longer one of your own. Students will hardly ever talk to other students under this system, the communication may be brisk and lively, but it will be in several sets of two-way traffic, student to tutor, tutor to student. An analysis of this sort of discussion usually reveals that the tutor talks almost all the time.

It is hard discipline as a tutor to keep your mouth shut, to listen, and to show signs of listening instead of talking. Most tutors are good at talking and especially enjoy talking about their subject. Not talking can be exquisite agony, as any experienced tutor will know.

Some tutors may encourage student contributions, but may set up what has accurately been diagnosed as a 'guessing-game'. The game is played so that the student can hardly ever win, as in this brief transcript from a class comparing two poems by Wordsworth. The atmosphere of the class was entirely friendly and informal.

Tutor: Well now, you've read the second poem again, I hope. (*Murmurs of agreement.*) One thing that struck me, one thing I'm wondering, did you see any striking difference between this poem and the last one we read?

Student 1: It's longer! (*Laughter and pause.*)

Tutor: Well . . . yes!

Student 2: It is that this poem is somehow more . . . well, not so personal, it seems to have less of Wordsworth himself in it?

Tutor: Yes. But I was thinking of something else.

Student 3: The language is not so rich? Fewer metaphors?

Tutor: Yes, a good point. That's certainly true. We'll look at that later. Anyone got any more ideas?

Student 1: I don't like it! (*Laughter.*)

Tutor: Any more bright ideas? (*Pause.*) Well, what I was thinking was that this poem is much more in the ballad vein, isn't it? It's reminiscent of the old simple Scottish ballads – can anyone tell us what a ballad is?

The tutor's views

In this situation the tutor has said in effect to the class, 'Now guess what I've got in mind?' The trouble is that there may be dozens of legitimate points of comparison between two poems, any one of which the tutor may have in mind. The class plays along for a while, then says or signifies by silence the equivalent of 'I give up', after which the tutor announces the 'answer'. Not only does this sort of technique suggest to a class that there is only one acceptable and right major point of comparison, it also suggests that responses to a poem have to be tackled in a particular order (the suggestion about metaphor was pushed aside for 'later'), and that it is the response the tutor has in mind which is the most important one. Such discussion technique ignores the possibility that students themselves can and should make fresh and direct contributions of a quality which would surprise tutors who think theirs are the only interpretations which count.

Guessing-games develop out of a confusion between 'real' discussion and 'question and answer'. There are subjects – mathematics, for instance – where it might be legitimate for a tutor to say something like 'Can anyone tell me what the square root of forty-four is?' because there is only one possible answer. It is surprising how few such subjects are, and at what a low factual and academic level they have to function for it to be possible to deal with them in so summary a fashion.

Tutors may press their own views in other, more subtle ways. They may reward someone who offers a view agreeing with their own by nodding vigorously or by saying, 'Yes, a good point', or by following it up with some forceful elaboration of their own. They may frown doubtfully at a student giving an opposite opinion, or simply by the coolness of their nod on receiving the comment imply that only courtesy prevents them saying that such a comment was ridiculous, or inappropriate. They may initiate the discussion and prod it along with leading questions, as in this sociology class (again the atmosphere of this particular class was noticeably relaxed and uninhibited):

Tutor: Don't you think society is still rather hard on never-married women who are also parents? We see this moral panic stuff over and over again, don't we?

Student 1: Well no, I think that's a bit *passé* now when you have so many famous women who've chosen it as a way of life.

Tutor: Even so, I think we all disapprove of someone breaking the moral code.

Student 2: Yes, and the children suffer because they never have a male role model.

Student 3: Well I'm a single mother and I resent the idea that my children are suffering.

Student 4: You can't apply this to individuals, it's the general social effect we're talking about here and I agree there's still the idea that the good old nuclear family is best. Single parents probably get discriminated against in all sorts of ways. My sister had a baby at 16 and my parents behaved as if the world had come to an end. They put really strong pressure on her to have an abortion because, in spite of everything, they still felt it was something 'people like us' didn't do.

Tutor: Yes, that's right. Why do you think that is? Is it that we all feel threatened by someone who doesn't conform? (*Nods of agreement.*)

The phrasing of the tutor's initial question has given the group a clue either to his own view, or to what he interprets as the common view of a familiar social problem. It may be that the tutor can offer the class evidence on how 'society' views single, never-married mothers – surveys, novels, articles – but he notably does not do this. He quickly tries to encourage the group to confess to prejudice themselves, and seizes on a personal anecdote told by one student as the occasion to drive home his point by virtually accusing the student who told it of prejudice herself. In such discussion the tutor gives it a gloss of freedom, but in fact he is seeking confirmation of his own view and moral standpoint (and in the extract quoted, eventually wins it superficially) almost as firmly as the tutor in the guessing-game.

The information and sources that tutors use for discussion may easily be chosen to support their own views. The group here is usually at the mercy of the teacher unless its members are lucky enough or enterprising enough to discover the bias for themselves:

> Between school and university I took a year's voluntary job, but to keep my hand in I thought I'd go to an extra-mural class in my own subject – history. It appealed to me because it was advertised as a course using original documents of the period, with lots of opportunities for discussion. It was very interesting and the lecturer was superb – a real enthusiast. I only discovered how incredibly partisan his view of the period was when in my third year at university I realized how his enthusiasm for one school of thought had totally affected the documents he gave us and the evidence we used for our discussions. He was quite unaware of what he had done, I'm sure.

The dangers of planning

Some tutors attempt to control a discussion by drawing up detailed plans for it in advance. Control can become manipulation where a tutor also tries to anticipate the content of the students' answers. It is fair enough to have a rough plan in mind and to have at hand the materials and information needed to explore the likely ramifications of the three or four questions any one class could be expected to explore in a few hours, but you should always be prepared to abandon this plan if the interest of the class points clearly in another direction. What seems a red herring to you may well be an absorbing topic to your students. Each red herring should be judged on its merits by the group as well as by you. It certainly seems a mistake to have too many rigid expectations about the length, content and likely conclusions of a discussion. In opening up discussion you are offering the class something free, floating and unpredictable. It is not possible to chart too closely in advance the form the discussion should take, for the essence of a valuable discussion is the unexpectedness and originality of the new territory which should constantly be explored. It is only when your students can see that you are genuinely offering them opportunities to speculate, think and interpret that new ideas will flourish.

A good discussion inevitably exposes the ambiguities and complexities of a topic. Many tutors, searching for a way to find a framework for their students that will hold widely diverging views, will attempt to impose a 'conclusion' on the discussion which can easily be a false representation of what has been said:

> It puzzled me at first, but I never recognized his summaries as accounts of what we had all said. After a bit I realized that the summary represented (a) his own opinion, (b) what he wished we had said. I think we must have disappointed him by not being such a bright class as he'd hoped. We certainly weren't up to his standards.

Paterson makes the same point from an educationist's view:

> One inevitably wonders how many . . . counterfeit discussions are staged in adult classes by tutors whose confidence in their own preferred views disables them from taking the

views of their students with the utmost seriousness required of all the participants in authentic educational dialogue. I am referring less to the assertive and dogmatic tutor than to the kind of tutor who unobtrusively and skilfully synthesises the various discussion contributions of his students, by judicious selection and emphasis, into a neatly structured and rounded proposition or body of propositions, which are then represented as the 'conclusions' of the 'class discussion' although they have in fact been evolved by the tutor, who has ingeniously utilised the discussion, always more or less under his discreet control, as an educational device for arraying precisely this body of propositions, deemed by him to be of some importance to his students at this stage of their classwork. The teaching skill exercised by such a tutor may be of a very high order, and the results gained may be of great educational value. To the extent that his students believe themselves to be participating in a genuinely open-ended dialogue, however, they are being misled; and to the extent that he believes himself to be 'conducting a discussion', he is misleading himself.[2]

It is, of course, your job to present a discussion to a group in such a way that members can see they have learnt from it, but it seems a false way to set about this delicate task by using phrases such as 'Well, I think we're all agreed that . . .' or 'Everyone seems to have come to the conclusion that . . .'. It is highly unlikely that all students are of one mind on any topic worth extended discussion, and it is your task to see that a false consensus does not emerge. You should encourage and maintain divergent views, even where they conflict sharply with your own. As Albert Mansbridge, founder of the Workers' Educational Association, said: 'The class is not intended for the passing of resolutions, but is rather a means whereby all relevant facts and arguments may be looked at and turned over'.

Core skills

To facilitate through discussion, you need a number of core skills, some more easily acquired than others.

Creating trust

Participants in a discussion have to feel safe. It has to be all right to say what you think without fear of attack, whether from tutor or other participants. The most certain way to achieve this is to behave in a way which models trustful behaviour yourself. There is no place in facilitation for sarcasm, put-downs, jokes at other people's expense, showing off your own superior knowledge, gossiping or clumsy interrupting.

It is vital to make some kind of contract with the group so that both you and they are clear about the *rules of the game*. This kind of learning may be scary for some people or simply unfamiliar. Say what you are prepared and not prepared to do and ask what the group wants from you. Explain the principles of discussion and also the behaviour that goes with it on both sides. Ask for questions and suggestions. In the early phases, it will be useful to write up your joint conclusions on a white board or flipchart so that conformance can be monitored by all of you.

Here are some ideas for a contract of this sort that I have found to stand the test of time:

- *One person at a time: one issue, one thought, one idea.* It is amazing how many apparently sophisticated groups in the work I now do find this hard. A colleague and I worked with a BBC team over a period of some time to help them build their team and improve their performance. At the beginning, there was such chaos when it came to discussion that we had to insist on apparently childlike rules (their suggestion). One of these was that anyone wanting to speak would first raise their hand. Yes, these were people in well-paid jobs, none of them younger than 35, but they still needed this elementary help in order to learn the useful discipline of only one person at a time speaking. At the start, you may have to work harder than feels comfortable to get people to refrain from:

telling anecdotes (in my street we . . .);
interrupting;
giving advice.

It is especially important to help people recognize how often they may be introducing their own agendas rather than working on an issue brought by someone else. Gently but firmly interrupting the flow and saying something like 'Whose agenda are we on now?' may help people learn to recognize what they are doing.

- *It is OK to admit to mistakes and uncertainties.* This is vital. You will be using facilitation and discussion because there are no clear right or wrong 'answers'. When this is the case, it is essential for people to be able to own up to what they don't know and feel uncertain about. You can lead the way here. If you make a mistake or are uncertain, own up.
- *Say 'I' when you mean 'I'.* It is surprising how often we say 'we' or 'people' when what we mean is 'I'. Challenge participants who resort to generalizations of this sort. Your group will soon get the hang of it and will realize how much better the discussion is as a result.
- *Give affirmation.* We all need affirmation, and some of us need more than others. Notice what people are saying and comment on it. Encourage others in the group to do the same. Use phrases like:

'That's an interesting idea';
'Going back to the point you made earlier, I can see that . . .'.

Watch out for being the only person in the group to do this. Show the group that it is a duty that should be shared.
- *Laughter and fun are good ideas.* A good laugh is essential to reduce tension and to defuse embarrassment. Aim for at least two good laughs per session.
- *Give frequent feedback.* A group that knows how to give frequent, skilled feedback is well on the way to accelerating its learning. Most groups do not give feedback, indeed they

shy away from it. It is easier to grumble in the corridor afterwards about how awful some other person in the group is. Modelling this behaviour yourself will help the group learn how to do it.

Listening with respect

Facilitation is about respect for each and every participant. It means being able to listen without judgement, even when you fundamentally disagree with what the other person is saying. It means listening without feeling the need to criticize, collude, blame or trivialize the other person's concern, and without trying to persuade them that your view is right and theirs is wrong. Your aim is to listen without trying to construct a theory in your head about what someone is saying. Your energy goes into the effort you are making in trying to hear them properly.

When you listen with respect, you give your whole attention to the other person. This is real attention not fake attention. You are fully present for them. Your effort goes into trying to understand properly what is in their heads rather than queuing to speak yourself. Beware of getting distracted by wanting to impress or to discharge some of your own anxiety.

Summarizing

If you do nothing else but this during a discussion, you will be doing a useful job. Listen for the main themes. Note the agreements and disagreements. Remember your role is not about drawing conclusions. It is about keeping track of the ebb and flow of the talk. Useful phrases here are:

- So to summarize where we are . . .
- It feels to me that a summary of the main lines of our discussion would be useful here . . .
- So what I've heard X and Y say is . . . and what I've heard A and B say is . . .

If you are getting confused yourself, it will be true in nine cases out of ten that the group is too. So say something like:

> Can anyone help me here? I'm getting confused about where we're going with the discussion at this point. I've heard X point and Y point made, but I'm a bit lost about what that's contributing . . .

Similarly, part of your role, certainly at the beginning of the group's work, will be to keep an eye on the time and to show the group that this is what you are doing. Sit where you can see a clock, or take off your watch and put it on on a table within easy glancing distance. Remind the group of how much time has been used, or is left. Here are some useful phrases:

- I notice we've been discussing this aspect of the topic for ten minutes. That seems like quite a lot to me, but how do you feel?
- Have we exhausted this aspect?
- We've got ten minutes before we break. Would you like to carry on with this topic or move on to something else?
- We've had an hour and a half. I've noticed that some people are looking a bit tired. Is it time for a break?

Questioning

Skilful questioning is essential for good facilitation. Some questions are more useful than others.

Questions to avoid

Double questions simply confuse people. For example: 'When you say you like working with computers, why is that? Is it any computer or are you more keen on the Mac?' In this example, there are two questions and the respondent will have to concentrate on remembering both halves of the question in order to reply.

Leading questions suggest the answer. For example, 'Have you thought that the Internet might be a good way to find this information?' The obvious answer is expected to be 'Yes', thus sparing the respondent the trouble of thinking for him or herself.

'Advice in disguise' questions are well meant, but again, prevent learning and create opposition in the hearer's mind. For example, 'When I faced this problem, I found that it helped me to take it very slowly. Don't you think you'd find the same?'

Avoid any questions that begin:

Is/isn't . . . ?	Have/haven't . . . ?
Was/wasn't . . . ?	Has/hasn't . . . ?
Does/doesn't . . . ?	Must/musn't . . . ?

Questions beginning this way are always advice in disguise. Try it and see.

Rhetorical questions are an even more obvious technique than leading questions. They suggest that only the most dim person could ever disagree with the thinly-disguised proposition in the question. For example, 'Wouldn't you agree that anyone who likes sixties music is a bit sad?'

Powerful questions

The most powerful questions are also the most difficult to ask. It takes practice and skill to avoid falling into any of the traps above. Remember:

- keep it short and simple;
- the ideal facilitator's question is no more than seven or eight words long.

For example:

So what do you think about that?
When that happens, what do you do?
What's your view?

Two even shorter questions which I often use are:

So . . . ?
Because . . . ?

An even more extreme version of this approach is to remain silent. If you just look encouragingly at the person who is trying to speak, nod and wait you may find you get surprising results. This technique can often help the under-contributor who struggles to find a place in the flow of talk.

The most useful questions for facilitators invariably begin with some version of the word *what*. A question beginning 'What . . . ?' obliges the respondent to find their own words and cannot be answered 'Yes', 'No' or 'Don't know'. Here is an example which compares an *advice in disguise* question with a *what* question on the same topic:

Would it be an idea to lose weight by joining a WeightWatchers group? (Advice-in-disguise. The questioner has already got his or her own idea about the solution to losing weight.)

Compare this with the far more open:

What are your ideas about how to lose weight?

Another useful question is one which begins 'Tell me . . . ?'

Clarifying and probing questions are also essential to effective facilitation. They are necessary because there will always be people who find it hard to make their meaning clear. This could be because they speak too little and are too cryptic in what they say, or because they are so verbose that they and everyone else loses the thread of what they are trying to say. With the cryptic speaker, try saying 'Say more about that . . . ?' With the garrulous person try saying 'So what's the bottom line point you're making here X . . . ?'

Seeing the patterns

Over the years I have been running discussions and facilitating events of all sorts and I have noticed many common patterns.

You need to be alert to these and other common phenomena because if you are not alert to them, you can't do anything about them. So watch out for:

- Men making assertions where women ask questions.
- Men talking more than women, unless it is a women-dominated group.
- 'Ping-pong' dialogues developing between facilitator and one or two participants.
- The person sitting directly in your eyeline speaking more than others.
- The people sitting directly to your right and left speaking least.
- People colonizing one seat with their coats and briefcases and returning to that seat constantly so that it becomes 'theirs'.
- People sitting next to those with whom they feel they have most in common. So, for instance, all the younger men may sit together, or all the people from the same department.

Where they continue for any length of time, such patterns can be destructive and will lead to dysfunction. They are dangerous because they exclude. Where you notice them happening, break them up by:

- drawing attention to them;
- sitting in a different place yourself, thus forcing change in the seating pattern;
- arranging the room to facilitate easy eyelines (see Chapter 3);
- refusing to play ping-pong;
- reviewing the group's process regularly. This means asking people how they feel about the discussion and also asking them to notice the patterns. Useful questions here are:

Who has spoken most?
Who has spoken least?
How do you feel the discussion has gone?
In what ways does this group remind you of others you are in?
What have you learnt from the way the discussion has gone?
What mark out of ten would you give the discussion for enjoyment?

What mark out of ten would you give it for usefulness?
What would help make this a better discussion next time?

Investment of emotion

Emotion comes even into judging facts and superficially more
neutral scientific subjects, as was interestingly shown by M.L.
Johnson Abercrombie in a classic experiment with medical students who, in one set of 'free' discussions (that is, with no
academic direction from a tutor), were asked to compare two
radiographs of a hand. The results showed how many unjustifi-
able assertions the students were inclined to make on sparse
evidence, how frequently they saw what they expected to see,
and how emotionally they would defend their conclusions:

> The inferences the students had made were not arrived at
> as a result of a series of logical steps, but swiftly, almost
> unconsciously. The validity of the inferences was usually not
> inquired into, indeed the process was usually accompanied
> by a feeling of certainty of being right, and consequently
> the discussion of incompatible views sometimes became very
> heated. Frequently the correct inference had been made (as
> with the statement that A was a younger hand than B), and
> then discussion did not change the formulation of the end
> results, but only brought to light the processes involved in
> getting it.[3]

This concern with evidence, with logical processes, with
the distinction between factual information and what can be
deduced from it, is the educational end which discussion is
superbly well equipped to fulfil. Abercrombie summarizes her
aim in the course of unguided discussions as being

> to make it possible for the student to relinquish the security
> of thinking in well-defined given channels and to find a
> new kind of stability based on the recognition and accept-
> ance of ambiguity, uncertainty and open choice.

This might well serve as an aim for most of the courses for
adults which use a discussion method as one of their tools.

The flow of resources

'Free' group discussion is sometimes denigrated as 'the pooling of ignorance', and, clearly, if discussion is to be more than this, the group must have a constant flow of new information and ideas. Traditionally these have come from the tutor, but you are as a tutor at the mercy of your own bias, probably as much in academic subjects as in matters of value judgement. In a course where there is no lecturing at all from the tutor and where the learning is done entirely through discussion, then your role becomes more concentrated on the flow of resources, many of which might be digested outside the class time: for instance, videos, novels, audio tapes or open learning texts. If you do not have the benefit of a ready-made 'multi-media' course you can still construct one – with the expense of more time, trouble and cost, of course – by establishing your own collection of documents, tapes and photographs, to which you and your group can constantly add. All discussion is demanding, but the more nearly it approaches an open exchange of views, the greater the skill it will demand of you.

Problems

Free discussion may solve some problems, but it undoubtedly creates others. For instance, some students are satisfied enough with a tutor who is willing to tell them what to think, and may be quite happy with the appearance and not the substance of discussion, simply because a substantial discussion in an educational setting may be unfamiliar as well as demanding. The only school experience of 'discussion' many people have may well be something close in spirit to the dismal process Charles Dickens satirized in *Hard Times* over 100 years ago, when he set the first scene of his attack on the cold spirit of utilitarianism in Mr Gradgrind's school during a visit by a 'government officer' – perhaps an earlier, grimmer version of a modern Ofsted inspection:

'Bitzer,' said Thomas Gradgrind. 'Your definition of a horse.'

'Quadruped. Graminivorous. Forty teeth, namely twenty-four grinders, four eye-teeth, and twelve incisive. Sheds coat in the spring; in marshy countries, sheds hoofs, too. Hoofs hard, but requiring to be shod with iron. Age known by marks in mouth.' Thus (and much more) Bitzer.

'Now girl number twenty,' said Mr Gradgrind. 'You know what a horse is.'

She curtseyed again, and would have blushed deeper, if she could have blushed deeper than she had blushed all this time. Bitzer, after rapidly blinking at Thomas Gradgrind with both eyes at once, and so catching the light upon his quivering ends of lashes that they looked like the antennae of busy insects, put his knuckles to his freckled forehead and sat down again.

The third gentleman now stepped forth. A mighty man at cutting and drying, he was; a government officer; in his way (and in most other people's too), a professed pugilist; always in training, always with a system to force down the general throat like a bolus, always to be heard of at the bar of his little Public-office, ready to fight All England. To continue in fistic phraseology, he had a genius for coming up to the scratch, wherever and whatever it was, and proving himself an ugly customer. He would go in and damage any subject whatever with his right, follow up with his left, stop, exchange, counter, bore his opponent (he always fought All England) to the ropes, and fall upon him neatly. He was certain to knock the wind out of common-sense, and render that unlucky adversary deaf to the call of time. And he had it in charge from high authority to bring about the great public-office Millennium, when Commissioners should reign upon earth.

'Very well,' said this gentleman, briskly smiling, and folding his arms. 'That's a horse. Now, let me ask you girls and boys, Would you paper a room with representations of horses?'

After a pause, one half of the children cried in chorus, 'Yes, sir!' Upon which the other half, seeing in the gentleman's face that 'Yes' was wrong, cried out in chorus, 'No, sir!' – as the custom is, in these examinations.

'Of course, No. Why wouldn't you?'

A pause. One corpulent slow boy, with a wheezy manner of breathing, ventured the answer. Because he wouldn't paper a room at all, but would paint it.

'You *must* paper it,' said Thomas Gradgrind, 'whether you like it or not. Don't tell *us* you wouldn't paper it. What do you mean, boy?'

'I'll explain to you, then,' said the gentleman, after another and a dismal pause, 'why you wouldn't paper a room with representations of horses. Do you ever see horses walking up and down the sides of rooms in reality – in fact? Do you?'

'Yes, sir!' from one half. 'No, sir!' from the other.

'Of course no,' said the gentleman, with an indignant look at the wrong half. 'Why, then you are not to see any-where, what you don't see in fact; you are not to have anywhere, what you don't have in fact. What is called Taste, is only another name for Fact.'

Participants accustomed to a tutor who seems omniscient may take time to find the courage to speak freely in a group, or to believe that their contributions really are being taken seriously. Indeed, after a while, when it is clear that they are being lis-tened to with scrupulous attention by tutor and other students, this may in itself be alarming. A participant who can throw in a frivolous comment in a discussion dominated by the tutor may be overwhelmed by the responsibility of speaking in a serious discussion where the emphasis is on the participants.

Others may resent it if you do not take a dominant role, and may attack you by saying something like 'You're the tutor, you've studied the subject longer than we have. Why don't you tell us?' This situation sometimes develops in a class where the tutor is clearly keeping something up his or her sleeve, and deceiving the class about his or her own opinion or holding back useful knowledge. I once watched a tutor, who believed in never under any circumstances giving his own view, attacked by an exasperated class after he had answered perhaps the tenth direct question from one of his students with 'I don't know, what do you think?' He received the tart and well-deserved response 'But you do know and you ought to tell us.' A colleague of mine described his 11-year-old daughter struggling with her homework and asking him how to spell 'chrysanthemum'. She then immediately followed this request with: 'And before you ask me how I think I spell it, please don't. I just want the answer!'

Discussion can often seem ragged and inconclusive, especially to students used to assuming one 'right' answer. These people may find the ambiguity of a discussion too trying, and many others will feel that 'just talking' is a waste of time. These students might share Professor Max Beloff's view that 'the don teaches the boy: he knows more', a view that denies the possibility that students can and frequently do surpass the master and learn from each other, especially when opportunities are made for them to do so, and when the skills of discussion are learnt by students as well as practised by the tutor. Nevertheless, many discussions can seem time-wasting, and with adult groups relying heavily on the discussion process you will find it essential to try various ways of consolidating the discussion. The possibilities will include notetaking, written work based on the discussion, or personal research undertaken as a result of points made during it, as well as progress reports, or discussions on the discussions.

This kind of work can also be the occasion for correcting the mistakes and factual errors inevitably made by students in the course of discussion. Mistakes you diagnose as 'dangerous' can properly be corrected in the classroom, but the responsibility for doing this need not always be yours. Usually there are plenty of students as capable of making the correction. Otherwise, a quiet word in private is usually more effective than a public reproof.

Conflict and argument

You are ultimately responsible for the mood and atmosphere of your group. Hectic, fevered discussion can arouse a priceless interest and excitement in a topic, and it does no harm to bring disputes into the open. Sometimes, however, discussions become so heated and the participants so involved that they become angry. Discussion can then be confused with argument, with one 'side' of a group ranged implacably against the other. The point of the discussion turns away from the educational objective of exchanging opinions, listening to and learning from other people, and turns instead into a battle where one side has to concede defeat and lose face:

> Every time the class met, although it was nineteenth-century social and political history we were discussing, the discussion always got round to politics today. We all knew Mr ____ was a keen Labour man because he was on the council. He didn't say it himself, but I felt he used to encourage one or two others to argue it out. Sometimes it got nasty and there would be name-calling, etc. On one occasion it was serious and one of his opponents was so angry he refused to come to the pub afterwards. I felt the tutor ought to have stopped it but it was hard to see what more she could have done other than try to keep the peace a bit better.

In a situation like this 'education' has gone. People who are encouraged to state extreme views with such vigour are well on the way to finding it impossible to listen to anyone else. Having committed themselves vehemently and publicly to one view, it becomes difficult to retract or to explore the possibility that other people may have a view which is equally valid. The point of discussion should not be to establish a majority view, or even any one range of views, but to develop understanding, to learn how to make up one's mind, how to assess evidence, how to formulate conclusions. The conclusion itself may well be an irrelevance. When you see argument rather than discussion developing you will do well to use your authority to cool the atmosphere with a joke or an invitation to examine some evidence, or to ask some other people to contribute.

It may be that some tutors are glad to see arguments develop because tutors tend to evaluate the discussions in their classrooms in terms of how 'stimulating' or 'lively' they are. Not all discussions need to be noisy or obviously vigorous to be educationally valuable. A good discussion may be quiet, apparently low-key, with a lot of thoughtful silences. Some tutors are afraid of silence and leap in to fill any pause that looks like becoming an embarrassment, perhaps because long silences have connections with social embarrassment. A class which has established that a pause can continue until someone is ready to fill it with a considered comment may well produce more measured and telling points than the hastier, superficial sparkle of a lively, non-stop discussion.

Tears

The more important the topic to the group, the more you can expect strong emotion from time to time. Inevitably, there will be times when someone gets upset and cries. Some tutors feel that this is the ultimate horror:

> I was running a course on fair selection for human resources staff in an organization. Put bluntly, it was about how to make sure that there were no embarrassing tribunals. About a third of the way through the day, we were dealing with practice selection interviews, and doing it through role-play. Suddenly, one of the participants burst into tears. It turned out that her partner was out of work and had been rejected for a job at an interview the day before. She was overwhelmed with worry about the mortgage and it was all too close to home. I just froze – I didn't have a clue what to do.

In my experience, it is rare to get much warning of such an occurrence. People can sit on their emotion for a long time and disguise their distress, but then it suddenly bursts out. The keys to coping are:

- stay calm yourself;
- do everything you can to preserve the other person's dignity;
- deal with the immediate distress; don't try to find out the underlying cause at this stage;
- ask the person what they would like to do;
- give them the option of leaving, if that is what they would prefer;
- with *great* discretion offer a hug or a comforting touch.

It is a mistake to assume that people are 'forced' or 'made' to cry. Crying is a choice, even if it is made at an unconscious level, so it is the responsibility of the person who has made that choice. Your responsibility is to react appropriately. It is also a mistake to assume that people will regret the crying or even feel embarrassed about it. The experience may be usefully cathartic, as this account shows:

> I was doing a counselling course because it's a skill I need to have at work. We were halfway through the course – it was a series of one-day events. The subject of bereavement came up, and I don't know why, during one of the practices where we were always told it was not a role-play and had to work with real issues, the subject of the death of my mother came up. She had died ten years before, but I found myself crying uncontrollably. My 'counsellor' was wonderful and so was our tutor. We stopped and the tutor came over and sat down quietly with me, just lightly touching my arm. No one else looked embarrassed, though some told me later that they had been. It was all handled really well and I felt wonderful afterwards – really 'lightened'. In retrospect, I realized that I'd never really grieved for her properly and that event started a useful healing process for me.

Individual contributions

In a good discussion most members of a group feel willing and able to speak when appropriate. Many of the anxieties of tutors and the grumbles of students concern the numbers of people participating in any one discussion. Three typical comments illustrate familiar situations:

> A lot of people there had been going to these classes for years. They knew each other and they knew the tutor, so no one else got a look in.

> My *bête-noire* was a man who would always try to prove me wrong at great length. He was being forced by his

organization to attend, so he always felt he had to show he already knew everything that I was teaching. He tried to dominate every discussion.

I always thought our discussions were good, but one evening for interest, I counted up the number who had said something. I was horrified to discover that only 6 out of 16 had said anything.

Even in a group where everybody contributes at some time, there will always be some who talk more than others. This can be a cause for concern if those who talk most are preventing other people from joining in, or are seeming to waste the group's time with rambling anecdotes, with harangues, or simply with information too difficult for the rest of the group to understand. Adult groups often contain one member who is more knowledgeable than the rest. You may find it tempting to engage one prominent student in discussion – sometimes simply out of pleasure in talking, sometimes because of a cowardly wish to placate someone who might otherwise become bored and restless. The short-term solution is to let him or her get on with it, but if you habitually allow one person to dominate a class you are only storing up trouble for the future. It is unfair to other people, who eventually become irritated and fidgety and may leave the class rather than sit through more sessions of a dialogue between a teacher and an apparently favoured student.

It is better instead to encourage people to develop self-criticism about the quality and length of their own contributions. You can set the pace by inviting the group to evaluate each other's contributions: 'Does anyone have a comment on that?' or 'What do other people think?' In a class where this capacity has been encouraged, participants are often able to interrupt a lengthy contribution either with challenges and questions, with comments of their own or, as I saw once in a philosophy class, simply with a good-humoured, 'You've had three minutes by my watch, time to let someone else in now!'

Nevertheless, dominant members of groups are often able and energetic people, whose initiative and enthusiasm can be valuable to the rest of the group, either in the ideas they contribute to general discussion, or in the extra research, short lectures and special assignments they may occasionally be encouraged to undertake. It is sometimes hard to keep a careful balance between letting them tyrannize a group, on the one hand, and letting them waste their talents, on the other. You may find that you can speak privately to an over-talkative student, asking him or her to talk less. This can sometimes be effective and may be the appropriate thing to do, but you run the risk of seeming impertinent or else suggesting a conspiracy between yourself and your specially clever student, with both of you agreeing to patronize the less fortunate slower people.

Silent members of a class, or people who speak only rarely in a discussion, can present problems when you do not want to bully people into speaking but also want to see everyone make some sort of contribution. People who do not speak can be silent as a way of showing disapproval of what the rest of the group are saying; they can be silent out of shyness or diffidence or laziness; silent because although they would like to speak, conditions never seem right for them to take the plunge; or simply silent because they prefer to listen to other people rather than to talk themselves.

You must judge each case on its merits. There is no evidence to equate participation in discussion with learning, and if people prefer to be silent it could be an impertinence to try forcing them to speak. Attempting to draw out a shy student by asking direct questions may face him or her with an excruciating ordeal and may, in any case, fail to produce a response. I remember a woman in one of my classes who simply stonewalled this attempt to be helpful by shaking her head silently and staring down at the table. Other people may feel you have provided them with just the opening they have been waiting for, but your effort will usually be more successful if directed more widely than at a single individual – 'Some of you have special knowledge of____. Would any of you like to say something on this?' Again, the rest of the group can be encouraged to look to each other for contributions, to get to know who has particular knowledge of or unusual opinions on some issue and can therefore be expected to say something valuable.

When a shy or less dominant member does make a brief contribution to a discussion, it is often helpful to rein in the discussion at that point to ask for further elaboration – 'It might be interesting if you expanded that point'. Alternatively, you can suggest a general pause in the discussion by saying something like, 'We seem to have covered a lot of ground rather quickly. Can we stop to think for a moment?' Focusing the discussion at one stage like this is often a useful way of allowing slower or more introverted thinkers to catch up and speak if they want to. There may be opportunities to do the same thing at the beginning and end of a discussion. I have seen some tutors encourage silent people to speak at these points by saying, 'We left a lot unsaid at our last session. Is there anyone who would like the last word?' Such invitations have, of course, to be followed by a generous pause otherwise they might just as well not be made.

Problems of over-dominant and too silent members can often be solved by splitting the group into smaller groups for some part of the class time:

> We start off as one group – about 15 of us – going over the week's written work, looking at a new poem or chapter. After coffee we divide into however many groups can be divided by three or four. Each group has a question written on a piece of paper. All the questions are closely related but different, and based on the topic we discussed before coffee. This takes 20 minutes, strictly timed. We then report back, compare questions, and have what is usually a most useful general discussion to finish off. With this system everybody who wants to can speak, and everyone is obliged to give really close attention to the text.

> There are 25 students, two tutors. We watch the video together, discuss it for ten minutes, then split. People who never speak in the large group normally say quite a lot in the smaller one.

It is not unusual for the first five minutes of the discussion to be the slowest and the most difficult to manage, and the part of the process that you may dread most. The best ways of encouraging discussion seem to be to ask people to prepare for it by thinking, reading and writing, to reassure them that silence does not matter, to make it clear that you really have withdrawn from your role of expert by saying 'Would anyone like to comment?' or some such phrase and no more. Most importantly, you must provide the group with an initial stimulus as emotionally gripping, or as intellectually intriguing and as complex, as possible. This could be a lecture, a dramatic reading, a film, a case study or simulation or anything else which demands an immediate response. Film and video are perhaps particularly useful in loosening tongues, as many people are used to discussing them informally without the strain that may be associated with academic discussion of a poem or book.

Remember, too, how much the shape of the room and the type of furniture (see page 70) contribute to atmosphere and eyelines. If your aim is a discussion which involves everyone, it is more or less essential to seat the group in comfortable chairs ranged in a circle, as that is the only way people can see or address each other easily. Where you have a group sitting lecture-style in straight lines, most people will only have one good view, and that is of you, so naturally they will be far more likely to address their remarks to you than to each other. The temptation to cap every student comment with one of your own will be almost irresistible.

Your role in discussion

Your role in an authentic discussion is, then, a taxing one. You must first of all make sure that the participants understand and share a common view of what discussion is by inviting them at the outset to discuss the discussion process, and by making it clear that your own role will be that of impartial facilitator rather than active teacher, of careful listener rather than frequent speaker. You must be ready to clarify issues so that groups understand what they are discussing, and why. You must be ready to relate the issues of one discussion to issues raised and explored on previous occasions. You must see that the group eschews personal attacks and violent sarcasm, as well as dull restatement of old prejudices. You must encourage and protect minority views. You should make sure that people learn to distinguish between fact and opinion, and be ready to feed in the resources which could supply facts and opinions giving an opposite, even an unpopular view. You must set the linguistic tone by using language everyone can understand. You must make sure that opportunities are kept open so that people who want to speak can speak. You must encourage the art of listening as well as talking.

If you can do all this, and at the same time train your group to take over these functions, too, you are offering your group a chance to learn in a unique way, by measuring minds and experiences with other people on equal terms.

The philosophical and democratic case for discussion, as well as by implication its educational justification, has never been made so powerfully as by John Stuart Mill in *On Liberty*, a case which can still serve as a model to any adult tutor today:

There must be discussion, to show how experience is to be interpreted. Wrong opinions and practices gradually yield to fact and argument; but facts and arguments, to produce any effect on the mind, must be brought before it. Very few facts are able to tell their own story, without comments to bring out their meaning. The whole strength and value, then, of human judgement, depending on the one property, that it can be set right when it is wrong, is that reliance can be placed on it only when the means of setting it right are kept constantly at hand. In the case of any person whose judgement is really deserving of confidence, how has it become so? Because he has kept his mind open to criticism of his opinions and conduct. Because it has been his practice to listen to all that could be said against him; to profit by as much of it as was just, and expound to himself, and upon occasion to others, the fallacy of what was fallacious. Because he has felt that the only way in which a human being can make some approach to knowing the whole of a subject, is by hearing what can be said about it by persons of every variety of opinion, and studying all modes in which it can be looked at by every character of mind. No wise man ever acquired his wisdom in any mode but this; nor is it in the nature of human intellect to become wise in any other manner.

Chapter 9

▶ Tutoring open learners

A tedious discussion at a recent conference I attended was a long and acrimonious wrangle about the differences between 'open' and 'distance' learning. It was tedious because these definitions are not particularly helpful to either 'experts' or learners. I shall use 'open learning' to describe any system where learners work alone, 'own pace, own place', on resources prepared by others, with minimal face-to-face contact either with tutors or other learners. This form of learning can come in many guises. The traditional correspondence colleges have always provided it. The UK has probably the most distinguished open learning institution in the world in The Open University. Many organizations have commissioned their own open learning material – for instance, one major financial company has its own suite of open learning materials for its managers. This provides basic material which is studied in advance of a face-to-face course. Now there is also a rapid expansion of e-coaching. This can be provided through a company's Intranet or from the Internet on a subscription basis.

Electronic communication of all sorts provides further staggering opportunities for new kinds of learning. Much of what traditionally was provided in person or by ordinary mail can now be done more effectively through electronic means. One major bank now delivers an enormous amount of its training through its Intranet, including training in customer care. Preparation for learning can now be done by email, with in-depth contact between the entire 'learning community' through bulletin boards and chat rooms. The learning itself may consist of projects which people carry out at set points and to be completed by agreed dates. The assessment is done through posting the results of your project to an email address. The group itself will never have met face to face, yet will feel as if the other members are old friends.

Electronic developments have created enormous interest in the learning and development community. However, we need to ensure that the current technology and all that will follow it does not become yet another false techno-dawn. I certainly remember the excitement of 'teaching machines' in the 1960s. This was followed by further excitement over 'programmed instruction' in the 1970s and interactive video and CD-ROM in the 1990s. All of these innovations failed to become mainstream. So far, only print endures as an alternative way of helping learners learn when they are not sitting right in front of you.

Now we have the situation where the ability of technology to deliver learning runs far ahead of our willingness or ability to catch up with it. The advantages of teacher and student being disconnected in time and space are huge: people being able to learn at their own pace, learning being delivered just in time and just enough, the savings on travel – and so on. Yet so far, the same old disadvantages apply: dependency on excellence in materials, the yearning for 'real' (i.e. face-to-face) contact, wilting motivation and the difficulty of finding time for learning in a busy life full of other commitments. This is why if you are dealing with 'open', 'distance' or electronic learners there is probably more that will unite them than will divide them.

Here, for instance, are some typical open learners:

- A young mother who dropped out of university to have her first child, now 3 years old. She is working on a creative writing course offered at a bargain price by a small college. She works on her assignments when her son is at playschool and sees the work as a low-key way of keeping her intellectual interests alive through the densely packed commitments of full-time motherhood.

- A 30-year-old who says he made a 'wrong turn' in his early twenties is studying to become a teacher in New Zealand. The entire programme is carried out by electronic means. This increases the chances that he will stay put in his remote community which urgently needs more teachers.
- A young man who left school at 16 and is now regretting that he did not continue his education. He is enjoying working as an accounts assistant in a small accountancy practice. The senior partner has encouraged him to work for qualifications and is paying half the cost of an open learning course for his Level 1 ACCA qualification. It is hard going to combine full-time work with studying and from time to time he toys with the idea of giving it up. However, if he passes the exam, he will probably feel motivated enough to go on to Level 2.
- A middle-aged woman working towards an A level in English through the National Extension College. Her motive is 'to acquire a decent certificate in a subject I've always loved'. She has never met her tutor. All their communication is on paper.
- A 45-year-old man in a senior role in a major public sector organization is in his fourth year of work with The Open University. He is strongly committed to getting an MBA. The organization is paying his fees. He describes his motivation as a mixture: 'wanting to be more professional' as a manager and 'vanity – I want those letters MBA after my name and now I've started it I've got to finish it!'
- A specialist professional in a financial services company has access to the organization's Intranet. They have a contract with a provider of open learning materials for open learning modules which will help people acquire the insurance qualifications they need to progress in the company. E-coaching is also available backed up by telephone coaching for people who get stuck.
- A nurse is working for a management qualification through a specially commissioned set of materials suitable for health professionals. Increasingly she sees her role as a nurse-manager, motivating and supervising other nursing staff rather than just a hands-on nurse who happens to be more experienced than others in her team. The course is giving her a new

set of ideas and insights but she is struggling with the assignments and urgently needs the boost that a summer school will give her.

These people show something of the extraordinary range of open-learning opportunities now available. Open learning is no longer the specialized province of degree work or a narrow band of professional qualifications, both perhaps in the past regarded as second best choices and often as second rate into the bargain. Open learning is now joining the mainstream in an unfussed way as a perfectly normal choice for some people in some circumstances. Perhaps the employer doesn't have trainers on the payroll, perhaps there are too few people at any one time to train simultaneously, perhaps the trainees are geographically scattered. Perhaps people missed out on some aspects of their education in youth, or it may just be that changing times and circumstances have created a need for updating, training or academic study.

But however different their subjects or circumstances may be, there are many ways in which open learners are likely to feel the same about their work.

Disadvantages for students

Before the advent of The Open University, correspondence tuition was notorious for its high drop-out rate. Colleges not unnaturally tend to be shy on the subject, but we know that on some of the more demanding courses, as few as 10 per cent of the initial enrolment survived to take the final examination. Even all the skill and care of The Open University cannot prevent roughly half the intake failing to complete its degree courses. All this suggests that students do not find open learning easy.

Some students are not 'joiners' by temperament. They relish working alone. It is probably more common, however, to find that solitary learning needs unlimited quantities of self-discipline:

I used to come home from work and set myself a target of two hours' studying. I was divorced by then so had no excuses. There was only me. However, there lay the problem.

I found myself infinitely distractible. I'd jump up and play the piano, or glance at a magazine, or find my hand straying towards the knob on the television set, or start planning the meal for the next day. When I was a schoolchild I used to find it boring sitting in rows with other kids, but at least the teachers kept you at it . . .

The support of other students is an element taken for granted in face-to-face teaching. Its absence in open learning can matter even to the most fiercely motivated:

Having missed out on proper higher education because of family problems I was absolutely determined to get what I felt I deserved through The Open University. I was completely ruthless about my time and didn't find it too much of a problem to get in the number of hours I needed. Even so, I longed to discuss and talk with other people tackling similar assignments. I couldn't get very often to the study centre – it was nearly 40 miles away and there was only one other student on the same course and I didn't rate my tutor too highly. One of the things that really sticks in my mind is taking a [study] unit to read on the long train journey to London once and spotting someone else with the same one! I was cheeky enough to introduce myself immediately and the time absolutely flew by. That was a real luxury: to talk science the whole time with a fellow student.

Working alone has other disadvantages: it tends to allow anxious students to become even more anxious. Adult learners are prone to nervousness anyway but in face-to-face teaching this can quickly be diminished both by sensitive teaching and by being with other students. In one wonderfully and unintentionally comic experiment, Pavlov, the distinguished Russian psychologist, found that if he performed a psychological test on a sheep, the mere presence of a second sheep made the first sheep less nervous. Common sense suggests that human beings are comforted in the same primitive way. A lone student easily develops a terror of showing his or her own real or imagined 'inadequacy'. It is common, for instance, for open learners to dread a tutor's judgement so much that they delay both starting and sending in their assignments. Many people spend two or three times the recommended number of hours on a piece of work, in painstaking and unnecessary reading and rereading. One of The Open University's first batch wryly commented:

> It's just as well I never have to admit the actual number of hours I spend on assignments. I'm sure I'd be told if I take the time I do I should never be taking the course.

That student spoke for hundreds of thousands of others subsequently whose experience was just the same.

Even in the classroom it takes all a tutor's skill and sensitivity to find the right ways of reassuring nervous students. It takes even more delicacy where the main means of communication is written. Face to face, a tough criticism can be softened and made acceptable by the way it is delivered. A tutor in the classroom may literally take his or her student to one side, may smile, may put one protective arm round them and then say 'Really ____, this essay won't do!' The tone will indicate that the professional criticism is meant to stand, but the smile, the gesture, the stance – the 'body language' in fact – will convey that no personal insult is intended. The identical comment written baldly down on an essay will have a very different impact – indeed it would take an unusually tough and confident student to remain unscathed by it. Written comment of this type is at worst withering for the recipient, at best infuriatingly ambiguous. In the classroom, at least there is opportunity to challenge a judgement on the spot; this is much more difficult for the open learner.

For lower-level academic work the inevitable emphasis on reading and writing in open learning has other disadvantages. It means the student must already be reasonably skilled and reasonably confident of their ability to cope with their own written work and with books:

> I can't describe the sweat of doing that first piece of work. I'd written reports – brief ones – but proper writing like this I hadn't attempted since I was 15. After working on it for

hours I showed it to my wife and she said it was fine. I looked back on it later and I was amazed how tactful she'd been, but I can tell you this, no piece of work I did later cost me so much in time and effort. And it was only half a page!

In some ways anxiety is likely to be worse the more highly motivated and able the student. Few adults undertake a demanding piece of learning 'for the sake of the subject'. Many want to learn skills which they can apply in their daily lives. Where open learning is concerned, one dominant motive may be the wish to gain a qualification. For some people, of course, this is simply a necessary and inevitable step in their career development. For many more, however, it is a way of proving their worth to themselves and to others:

> I am a housewife with three young children and typical of so many I suppose in that I felt my brain stopped working when I had my first child. I did the course to prove to my husband and his friends that I was not just a meal-provider and nappy changer. It did them (and me) and the children so much good to see me sitting at a desk with books. It was very hard going and very lonely at times as I had to give up my local class. I worried terribly about failing, as that would have been thoroughly mortifying. I just had to get that O level after telling everyone I was doing it.

Adults, like this student, prefer open learning because it allows them to fit their academic work around their other commitments. But this, too, can create problems if the course becomes so intensely involving that pressures build up too much for comfort. There is a limit to the number of potatoes which can be peeled while simultaneously reading a set book; there is a limit past which lunch hours cannot be stretched to rough out assignments. Open learners frequently become over-tired and over-stressed as a result. Some women, for instance, may start a guilty frenzy of extra housework to prove to their families that domestic life will go on yet more perfectly than before; some people may simply find both academic and other commitments utterly overwhelming and may make a mess of both.

Isolation, anxiety and a failure to control the pace of work successfully are particular problems with those open learners who have not undertaken a substantial piece of learning for some time. They tend to have lost (or sometimes have never acquired) the skills of studying. They may, therefore, spend hours reading every word of a book which only needs to be scanned; they may attempt laborious verbatim recording where sketchy notes would be more appropriate. In face-to-face teaching you can spot such problems and take remedial action. Where the bulk of the learning must be conducted through written material these difficulties may remain submerged, to the point where tutor and student alike become discouraged and defeated.

Disadvantages for tutors

Most of the problems for students have their parallels for tutors. Tutors, too, tend to be isolated. They may also be undertaking open learning work because in theory it can combine with other commitments, yet find in practice that it becomes very demanding. Such teaching is rarely lucrative, and it is much more difficult for the tutor to achieve one of the main satisfactions of the teacher's job: getting to know students and to observe their development. Accurate diagnosis of a student's difficulties is often reduced to guesswork when the only clues are written ones. Conventional teaching, even to tightly organized syllabuses, also usually allows teachers an enormous degree of freedom to develop their own materials and methods. In open learning this freedom is largely absent. The materials, the marking system, the methods, will already have been laid down. In some ways, the more efficient, caring and conscientious the system, the less impact individual tutors will be allowed to have on it. This cry from the heart is made by Pauline Kirk, an early part-time tutor for The Open University:

I find myself affected by an increasing intellectual loneliness. My work for The Open University takes up so much of my time and energy, yet who knows, apart from my students?

If I grade out of line the computer will pick up my aberration, or if I write too few comments my staff tutor will phone me tactfully, but in neither case will a central academic understand or care. I am infinitely replaceable . . . the part-timer's teaching duties are regarded merely as the assessment of, and support for, a centrally designed programme . . . In The Open University, then, one has a situation unique in British education – the existence of a large part-time teaching proletariat and a small academic ruling class.[1]

Advantages

In spite of all these difficulties, the benefits of open learning for both tutor and student are considerable. First, the learner is at the centre of the action. The best open learning materials will involve the student 'internalizing' a uniquely-tailored 'package' which is a close match to his or her circumstances. The learner controls the pace: for instance, a 30-hour course can be done in one intensive week, if you really want to, or spread over a year if that suits you better: you are not forced to keep time with other people. Even the apparent 'loneliness' of learning may have its appeal. Initial (unpublished) research done in the 1980s showed a large number of those questioned had a strong preference for learning alone and a positive distaste for the company of other students or human teachers. The best open learning materials will offer learners the best there is, the most up-to-date theories, the liveliest minds, and a commitment to interactivity which would put much face-to-face teaching to shame. The materials are portable and can fit in with other responsibilities. Work for my own Open University course was done as often on buses and trains or in the office as it was in a quiet room at home.

With vocational courses there is a further advantage: you are not cocooned from 'reality' while studying. Indeed 'reality' will probably be an important part of your course: important, for instance, in management training where many people have found that resolutions made on training courses to turn over new leaves begin to fade when back with all the demanding distractions of the real world.

Judging the quality of the course

Before committing yourself as a tutor of open learners, you may want to think carefully about the quality of the materials. A poor set of course materials can put you in the invidious position of having to endorse a product of which you disapprove. Better to scrutinize the course in advance and, if you dislike it, to decline the offer to work on it rather than to find yourself undermining the learners' motivation by subtle sniping or faint praise.

Good-quality open learning materials will usually have all the following features:

- Objectives written in testable and 'behavioural' terms (i.e. expressed as things the learner will be able to *do* closely linked to the skills needed for the task).
- Objectives stated for each unit or subsection.
- Simple, direct language which avoids sexist or racist stereotypes.
- An interactive style where the learner constantly has to contribute answers to 'problems', carry out tasks and projects, draw up action plans, supply personal interpretations and solve puzzles.
- Variety in the tasks the learner is asked to complete.
- Comments and answers to test questions which oblige learners to draw on their own experience.
- Feedback on the learner's 'answers'.
- High-quality professional design: large print, pleasing use of white space, colour and illustrations; enough space to write 'answers' comfortably; ability to open the workbooks flat.
- Material presented in 'timed' chunks of not longer than two hours.
- Assessment (e.g. self-assessment questions) closely linked to the objectives.
- A summary at the end of each unit.
- A course index.

- Sturdy binding and packaging.
- Variety in and appropriate use of media: print alone *may* be enough, but some audio-visual variety is usually both desirable and necessary. Audio, video, CD-ROM or website materials should be professionally produced to a high standard.

There is now much open learning material available which triumphantly meets all these criteria. However, there is also an awful lot of which does not. I was once proudly shown a text by a company which claimed it produced excellent open learning materials. The pages on display were already leaking out of a ring binder which was too small, and looked just like a set of lecture handouts. I commented mildly that it didn't look much like open learning to me. 'Ah,' they said, 'but look, there's plenty of white space at the top and bottom of the pages!' White space at the top and bottom of the page is most definitely not what quality open learning is all about.

Apart from visual dullness and lack of professionalism in design, there are two other common flaws in poor-quality open learning material. One is the failure to realize that every word must count. Many producers give in to the temptation to write lengthy bookish paragraphs. It should be impossible to skim-read an open-learning text; it should be designed to be 'worked through', not 'read'. The other common flaw is pitching the language at the wrong level – normally too high for the target audience. Sometimes this is because the authors wish to pander to what they see as the academic snobbery of those who have commissoned them; sometimes it is a straightforward failure to realize that many people will simply be baffled by the casual and unexplained use of words like, for instance, 'androgyny' or 'transmogrification' (I encountered both of these recently in open-learning courses allegedly aimed at people with no higher education).

The task of tutoring

In conventional teaching, as a conscientious tutor you will try to develop a whole battery of skills: those of the teaching methods specialist, group manager, resource manager, counsellor, subject specialist, setter and evaluator of work. It is this formidable array of roles which makes teaching such an extraordinarily complex and demanding job. Most open learning tutoring, however, requires both less and more than this. Of course, tutors must be specialists in their subjects, but most of your efforts must be concentrated on developing the skills of coaching and evaluation. Furthermore, these must be practised in written form. This is not at all the simple matter it may appear to teachers used to scrawling a few hasty marginalia on the scripts of students they also see face-to-face. Open learners, with all the disadvantages described earlier in this chapter, are peculiarly vulnerable to ill-considered written comment but are at the same time usually well able to judge the quality of a tutor's evaluative skill, as these quotes show:

> My comments this year have been extremely short, have criticised me on points specifically raised and no others and have thus been frustratingly useless. . . . I feel comments should be made not just on a personal basis, e.g. 'surely not *that*', or 'dynamic' underlined and 'natural' put in, but on a more general level too – about *doing* literary criticism and how I could specifically improve my work and my grades.

> First of all I look for encouragement, this always give me a boost to do better! I look for constructive criticism and keep this in mind to work from. I would always readily appreciate a more general criticism showing plainly if I was taking the wrong approach to the studies, or the specific question. I feel that this kind of help could quite possibly save a student a whole year's work.[2]

What, then, is the best strategy to follow? The extremes are easily avoided. Few tutors would need to be told that it is inexcusably arrogant, not to say vituperative, to write 'You are suffering from intellectual paralysis', as indignantly reported by one student. Nor would many fall into the opposite trap of the tutor who said ruefully of her own performance:

I am so terrified of apparently giving insults that I hardly dare write anything critical. My marks are always too high until exams loom up – then I panic. I know it's not fair but I'm afraid of hurting my students by 'honest' criticism.

Basic guidelines for giving open learners feedback

The basic guidelines have to be much the same as for giving any feedback in learning. The only difference is that much of it (perhaps all) has to be given in writing and every word must be weighed because that is what will happen to it when it is received by your learners.

- *Praise the positive first.* 'You have really understood the main points that Units 1 and 2 are making . . .'.
- *Keep it objective.* 'It might be better to have started the assignment with your second paragraph as this has much more "punch"' is better than 'I didn't like your opening paragraph'.
- *Be specific, be clear; give reasons* for praise or criticism. Wherever possible, comment should be full and unambiguous. There is no place in open learning for the inscrutable ticks, mysterious interrogatives and baffling exclamation marks which may appear on a script, whose author the tutor will see in the classroom. Allusive comments are also unhelpful. Face to face, you can explain what you meant by the cryptic words 'Jane Austen!' or 'Tawney!' in the margin. An open learner will all too probably be left guessing.
- *Give feedback quickly.* Return assignments within a few days: the effort will be fresher in the learner's mind and your comments will therefore have more impact.
- *Keep it succinct and appropriate.* Your own experiences, quotes from theories at a much more advanced stage . . . these are all distractions. Stick to the main points.
- *Be restrained with negative criticism.* Students need to have straightforward factual errors corrected in their work. A mis-

taken response is in any case harder to eradicate from an adult's than from a child's mind and the sooner it is put right the better. Even so, a page which comes back disfigured by a smallpox rash of negative red markings is horribly discouraging; it is always better to refer learners to the original sources which they can then check for themselves. When people's work is persistently full of mistakes, this always calls for investigation. Perhaps they have short-term special difficulties; perhaps they need intensive remedial teaching; perhaps they should not be on the course at all.

As with all good teaching, you must show that you understand and identify with the student's point of view. A tutor who with strident triumph writes 'No! No! No!' on a student's work shows insensitivity as well as bad manners. Adult students are both easily put down by such comment and also inclined after an interval to reassert their own values and self-confidence: in other words, no learning can take place from such a negative exchange.

More subtly than this, you need to write comments which deliberately acknowledge that you have absorbed what the student was trying to achieve. For instance, 'I see that you have thoroughly read X's book and I agree with your comments on his general theories. However, when you come to Z I think you should reread his section on Y where you may come to the conclusion that . . . Most authorities feel that . . .'. A tone like this, which perhaps seems at first contrived and tentative, nevertheless allows the student to retain his or her self-esteem, flatters by showing that the tutor has taken him or her seriously and yet still allows space to reconsider the original judgement. Genuinely friendly, open and hesitant comments which do not appear to close off further discussion have another advantage, too. They may allow both tutor and student to elevate their relationship to the status of an honest and absorbing dialogue, a continuing conversation rather than the snap and crackle of a boss–subordinate relationship, with all the resentful or craven submission that usually involves. Students who are on the receiving end of closed comments may also start trying to perform to rule, by simulating the kind of approach they come to believe will keep the tutor satisfied. The learning people accomplish under such conditions is nearly always bogus since it has not truly engaged either their minds or their emotions.

On the other hand, tutors who can develop the true dialogue approach can refine it to considerable effect. Teachers rated 'outstanding' by their students have at least one quality in common – they convey an ebullient and infectious enthusiasm for their subject which in itself is a tremendous stimulus to students. This quality is rare and it takes skill to convey that creative zest through words. Nevertheless, it can be achieved, as shown in this quote from an NEC (National Extension College) student, who wrote admiringly of her tutor:

> She never overwhelms you with new concepts, but her great gift is to tempt you with some dazzlingly interesting thought/book/newspaper article just at the time you're most ready to accept it. She gives the impression that she lives, breathes and sleeps her subject. I so look forward to getting my work back – it's like getting a particularly challenging and interesting letter from a friend now!

- *Be prepared to look underneath specific difficulties for underlying problems.* Spotting symptoms is easy, knowing the cause is far more demanding. Students who naively copy out whole paragraphs from a set text without acknowledgement may not be unintelligent, devious or foolish. They may just be ignorant of the academic conventions of quotation. Students who have clearly only consulted one out of several suggested sources for an essay may not be either lazy or stupid. They may simply not know how to fillet a book quickly.

How much you can help with such problems depends to some extent on how much your employing organization can tell you about the learner. Most will supply you with the learner's biography and will expect you to send a matching one of your own to the student. You should be encouraged to make contact: by telephone, letter or email. If you are tutoring someone inside your own organization then much more may be possible.

You will certainly be expected to keep scrupulous records of progress, and may also be required to help learners negotiate a realistic timetable for completing assignments (though not in The Open University, where there is usually a set timetable for each course).

The disadvantages of this kind of learning are immeasurably offset by building-in human support. This can take many forms. Traditional face-to-face support can consist of tutorials, self-help groups and summer schools. Today these can be easily augmented by electronic tutorials: 'asynchronous seminars' where learners can log-on 24 hours a day; email; and bulletin boards.

Where electronic means are concerned, the tutor becomes more like a moderator or facilitator, providing an online focus for conferences and seminars. This means understanding the needs of adult learners, being able to demonstrate sensitivity and maturity, having all the skills of facilitation backed up by excellence in writing ability, confidence in understanding and using the software, plus fast, accurate keyboard skills. This is a new blend of old skills. At the core, however, the electronic environment demands the same high standard: learners first. The learner must be at the heart of the e-environment. Without that, as with other kinds of learning, it can only fail.

Chapter **10**

▶ Coaching and mentoring

When the pupil is ready, the teacher will appear.

(Chinese proverb)

What's your image of a *coach*? Is it someone frustratedly chewing gum in the dugout and barking orders at their players? Is it a schoolteacher working with bored children to get them through their GCSEs? Both of these are common uses of the word, but increasingly it's being used in a very different way. When I coach, I am working with people one to one, and my aim is to release their own resourcefulness. They are people who want to get to the next level of effectiveness – as decided by them, not by me.

As someone interested in adult learning you will have many opportunities to coach. For instance, when someone on your course gets stuck at the same place time after time:

> I was teaching garden design and one of my students kept coming to me for suggestions about planting schemes. I began to realize that I was doing all the work and her learning about planting was nil. I went on a course myself about using coaching techniques and realized that this could be the answer. Next time she approached me with her request, I said 'Right, let's do some different thinking here. What are *your* ideas about what this garden needs?' At first I just got a blank look, but slowly her own ideas began to come out and we ended up with a much more confident garden designer! By not coaching, I was actually undermining her confidence, though of course my intention had been the exact opposite.

Alternatively, you may want to incorporate a coaching approach in all your teaching. In my own work with groups, this is increasingly what I am doing. However, I also now spend at least half my professional time working one to one with people in organizations as their coach. I meet them for two hours at a time over a period of a few months. Six sessions is about the average. They are usually too senior to go on courses either because they have already done all the courses their organization offers, or else they are reluctant to spend days at a time away from the office. They see coaching as a way to get targeted and confidential help in the areas where they want to make fast changes to their effectiveness.

Coaching has a literally infinite number of possible applications, but some ways you might use it include helping people to:

- recover their interest and motivation after a crisis of some kind;
- make decisions about whether to follow one path or another;
- learn how to learn;
- resolve a problem;
- undertake reviews of their careers;
- make decisions about life direction;
- understand themselves and the important people in their lives (work or home or both) so that their relationships are more enjoyable and productive;
- acquire skills;
- develop their creativity.

Maybe your interest in this area is because you have been asked to be a *mentor*. The word 'mentor' comes from the Greek legend where the learning of a young son was entrusted to the care of an older, wiser man. Many organizations now run mentoring schemes where the accumulated wisdom of an older person is made available to someone younger. Where the mentor uses a coaching approach, this can be a wonderfully powerful stimulus to learning. I shall use the two words as synonyms in this chapter because when a mentor coaches, he or she is far more powerful than when in the traditional mentoring role of just passing on advice.

Many people who are now working as coaches have a teaching or training background. They want to help people develop. However, when you coach in the style I am describing in this chapter, the process is different in a number of ways from conventional teaching. For a start, you do not need to be a subject expert. Your expertise is in the process of coaching, not the subject. It is even more a partnership of equals than other kinds of adult learning. You have no curriculum. The potential arena for discussion can include deeply personal matters as well as 'technical' skills. An example will make the point:

> James had just failed to get 'his' job after a merger between his NHS Trust and their neighbouring Trust when he came to me for coaching. Aged 46 and still feeling youthful and energetic, his bounce concealed a good deal of worry. Not only had he failed to get the chief executive job in the merger, he had also been shortlisted for, but had failed to get, two other senior chief executive jobs. He confessed that his confidence was rocky. His initial request was for interview coaching. 'I can obviously get on shortlists,' he said, 'but it must be my interview technique that's letting me down.' Resisting the temptation to go straight to interview coaching as the solution to his problems, instead, we spent the first session looking at James' whole life. On a scale of 1 to 10, how satisfied did he feel with his work, his marriage, his environment (home and work), the amount of fun in his life, family and friends?
>
> This apparently simple set of questions revealed a great deal of other information. James described himself as 'hating' the house where he lived and said that his marriage was not in a healthy state. His wife resented the apparent sacrifice she had made in giving up a career to bring up their children, and loathed living in the country. He did still love his work and wanted to continue with a health service career, but he had serious doubts about working in a large acute Trust.
>
> In that first session I also worked with James to help him acquire more effective questioning techniques so that he

could return to his boss and ask again for feedback about his interviews. His homework was to come to the second session having had this conversation and two others with people who had seen him at interviews and also to use the same techniques with his wife to find out what she really wanted – from their relationship and from her environment.

The effect was startling. At our second two-hour meeting, James reported back. Using the new style of questioning had revealed that where he saw himself as modest, he was coming across at interview as arrogant and confrontational. It was clear that James saw a job interview as a kind of oral examination – a place where you had to show off how much you knew about your subject rather than an essentially social occasion where people were deciding whether or not they could work with you. Videoing a practice interview was all that James needed to see himself as others saw him. 'Who *is* that prickly man?' he said, cringing as he watched it.

He said he and his wife had had their best conversation for years. Neither of them wanted to stay in the country and they had resolved to sell their house and move to an urban environment, assuming he found another job.

This tale has a happy ending. James had some further coaching in presentation and interview skills, giving him practice in presenting himself in a different way and learning how to give crisp, friendly answers to all the obvious questions that interviewers were likely to ask. He applied for and got a job running a different kind of hospital in an inner-city area. His wife started a small business which she ran from their new city-centre home. He reported their marriage as having a new lease of life.

There are several points to make about this story. One is my assumption that a client's personal life will be just as important to the coaching as their work life. If clients see my questions about their personal lives as impertinent, then they can refuse to reply, though perhaps one client in 500 ever does. Another is that the presenting issue, '*help me with interview technique*' was only one part of the problem. My coaching would probably have been far less effective if I had taken the client at his initial word. The coaching was a mutual process of exploration about what was holding James back. Finally, there was some recognizably 'technical' content in it where I helped James acquire skills he lacked. Mostly, however, with this client, as with so many others, he had all the important answers himself. He just needed the time, the space and the coaching relationship in order to find out for himself what he needed to do.

The Being and Doing Selves

In coaching we are looking at both the Being Self and the Doing Self. The Being Self is the core person: who we really are, how we feel about ourselves, our deepest commitments and values, how our earlier lives have made us what we are, our relationships. The Doing Self is about the skills we bring to our tasks, our work roles – our visible, public face. It is the Doing Self that usually presents for coaching. *'I need this or that skill. Will you help me?' 'I've got a new job and I'm finding it difficult.'* But as in the example I have quoted of James, the Doing Self may not find the answers to the problems until the Being Self is also engaged. Sometimes, the Doing Self is being compromised because the Being Self has been allowed to wither.

People will come forward for coaching when there is pressure for change in either arena. For instance, there may be pressure at the Being arena: marital problems, ageing, redundancy, illness. Or there may be pressure from the Doing arena: a boss who demands better performance, a change of job which needs different skills, and so on. Often there is a mysterious lack of progress in the Doing arena, in spite of teaching, mentoring and advice. The reason may be that the Being Self has not been engaged. When you coach, you give yourself and your client permission to work with both.

You may be wondering whether 'coaching' is just another word for counselling or psychotherapy. I don't believe that it is, but let's look first at what they have in common. All start from the assumption that it is desirable to have what the great American writer and thinker in this area, Carl Rogers, described as 'unconditional positive regard' for the client. There is no place for judging, sarcasm or sneering in coaching. If you don't or can't have respect for your client, then don't coach him or her.

Psychotherapy and counselling also assume that clients have the resources to solve their own problems. Coaching does too. There is a foundation in all three of knowing how to listen and ask questions.

Within these basics, there are some subtle and some large differences. Where the assumed state of the client for coaching is stability, a counsellor or therapist is more often dealing with a client in crisis or one who is facing serious long-term mental disorder. A counsellor will assume that their role is helping the client find a solution to an immediate problem. A psychotherapist's concern is with emotional healing, hence the amount of time spent looking backwards – especially at childhood. The language is significant. The word *therapy* means healing and psychotherapists talk about *patients*. The underlying model is clearly doctor–patient.

I had a vivid insight into this a few years ago when I sought psychotherapy after a deeply unsettling bereavement had left me with perpetual feelings of loss and anxiety. My psychotherapist called himself Dr—, although I knew his doctorate was a PhD in psychology. He worked out of a smart medical practice and for all the world it was just like going to the family doctor. He sat on a higher chair at a desk (sideways, but it was still a desk) while I sat on a long low sofa – a very nice sofa, but so low in comparison with his chair that I felt almost as if I was sitting at his feet. As therapy, this was not a success and after two sessions I had had enough and felt that my problems were untouched.

There are certainly grey areas. For instance, there are coaches who act as therapists and counsellors and therapists who also coach. But in general, the differences are important. My emphasis as a coach is on the future, on learning and on action. When I encounter a client who has some unresolved stuff from the past, I know my boundaries and refer them to one of several good psychotherapists whom I now know. The relationship between coach and client is most definitely one of equals. Coaches do not pose as experts except on coaching. There are no 'schools' of coaching as there are in psychotherapy, though it is possible that some may emerge as the profession matures and grows.

Giving advice

It's very easy to confuse coaching with advice-giving. Here are some typical situations:

> A young client asks you about a project she is working on. She knows that you have more experience in the subject of the project and says to you, 'What would you do?'

> You can see that a client is getting into difficulties with his drinking. You know from working with others in the organization that he's in the pub every lunchtime and there again after work. People are beginning to talk about the smell of beer that hangs around him.

What does a coach do? The easy answers are:

- Tell the young client how you would solve the problem – after all, she has actually asked you for your experience hasn't she?
- Tell the client with the apparent drinking problem that drinking is damaging his health and his reputation. He should control his alcohol intake and if he can't do that, then he should get some professional help, for instance from Alcoholics Anonymous.

But let's look a little more closely at what would be likely to happen in reality. With the young client, she gets her answer and the problem appears to be solved. But in the longer term, several less desirable things could also happen. First, she has not done any thinking of her own on the subject. Second, you are reinforced in her mind as the person with the answers, and her own ability to develop has been curtailed.

With the drinker, it is unlikely that he doesn't already know that he has a problem with his drinking. He is likely to be miserable and worried about it and about whatever has caused the resort to drink in the first place. Giving him advice may simply mean that he does his drinking in less public places and denies the problem in his sessions with you.

So as opportunities for coaching, it is probably safe to say that neither of these interventions is likely to be successful. You may feel better, but the underlying issues have not been touched.

Think about something you do yourself which is not wise, such as not getting enough exercise or smoking. Now imagine that a friend is giving you the standard advice on whatever you have chosen. For instance, if it is smoking, your friend might tell you that every cigarette shortens your life by five minutes, that smokers are twice as likely to develop heart, lung and circulatory disorders and that smoking is highly antisocial. How does this advice make you feel when you have had it in real life? Have you ever had advice of this sort which has produced a change in your actual behaviour along the lines suggested by the advice? The most probable answer here is 'no'.

Responses to advice

Advice does not work as a coaching tactic for these reasons:

- It suggests that the coach is wise and sensible while the advice recipient is a rather sad case who cannot get their life together; in reality coaches may have as many problems in their lives as clients.
- It undermines the essence of the coaching relationship as a partnership.
- The client's energy gets focused on repelling the advice rather than on dealing with the issue itself. This leads inevitably to the *Why don't you . . . ? . . . yes but* game:

  Why don't you get more exercise? It would really help you to reduce the stress.
  Yes, I agree it would be a good idea but I haven't really got time at the moment.
  OK, why don't you cut down the hours you work?

Yes, I'd like to, but my boss won't be satisfied with less than the amount of time I'm giving now . . .
And so on and so on.

- It discourages people from taking responsibility for themselves. If they take your advice, then it is your ideas that they are following.
- It does nothing to develop people's resilience and resourcefulness.
- If they take your advice and it goes wrong, then it becomes your 'fault'.
- It is unlikely that you will be telling the other person anything that they have not already thought of for themselves. For instance, advice on health and lifestyle issues is all very widely available. The reasons that people smoke and drink unwisely have little or nothing to do with non-availability of information.

So, when we give people advice it can come from wanting to avoid the pain of getting to the heart of the issue with the other person. It can also make us feel wise and helpful when it is possible that we are neither. Wanting to give advice can happen for good and bad reasons. The positive reason is that we want to be helpful. The less worthy reason is that we want to control the other person through the mechanism of giving advice.

Other traps

There are other traps in giving advice. The first is our tendency to read our own biography into what other people are describing:

Give me some advice on how I ought to deal with my boss.
Oh yes, I remember when I had a difficult boss, I . . .

The problem here is that you are you and there is no way you can ever know what it is like to be the other person. Your responses were yours alone. The truth is that you can't be the other person and can never know what it is like to be them.

Advice-in-disguise

It is also possible to do pseudo-coaching where what you are really doing is giving advice in disguise. So watch out for phrases like:

If I were you I'd . . .	Have you thought of . . . ?
When this happened to me I . . .	Another client of mine tried . . .

Advice and information

With executive coaching and other situations where you may have expert knowledge that it is useful to pass on to the client, a variant of the same principles will apply. Think of this as useful information which you want the client to have. The client still makes the decisions about whether or not to use it.

Offer your information (this may for instance be in handout form) as *one possible way* of looking at the problem. Talk it through and stress that these are basic approaches, which will not always work for everyone in all situations. Ask the client:

How does this strike you?
What seems useful and what seems not useful?
Which parts of this, if any, could you apply?
How could you apply them?
What will need to happen to make this real?

This approach works even in sports coaching, the one arena where you might think that expert input was truly necessary. In practice, many of us in coaching would claim that a good sports coach does not need in-depth knowledge of the sport. This radical claim can be backed up in a number of ways. For instance, the Israeli Olympic champion Mark Spitz was coached by someone who could not swim. The distinguished tennis coach Timothy Gallwey says that the real opponent in tennis is not the person on the other side of the net, it's the person inside your head. He ran both tennis and ski schools using coaching principles which started from the assumption that what you need to cultivate to be excellent at any sport is the most acute and intricate self-observation and awareness. The coach's role is to help the player acquire this. His tennis schools were so successful that he could not meet the demand for coaches. One year he brought in ski instructors trained in his methods. They wore tennis gear and carried racquets with strict instructions that the racquets were to stay firmly tucked under their arms. Their students were just as, if not more successful, than those of the tennis experts!

You can try this principle for yourself with a simple experiment that we use on our own coaching training courses. Ask a willing guinea-pig to help you. This person is the coachee. Give them some foam or tennis balls and ask them to aim the balls into a bin placed at increasingly large distances away from them. Your role as coach is to stand at the side of the coachee and to ask them to consider exactly what happens at each throw. How did it feel? What was the emotion at each stage? What was the level of concentration? What was the arm doing? What was happening to the eye? What makes the difference between a successful and an unsuccessful throw? Asking these questions quickly raises self-awareness and soon most people can reliably throw the ball accurately every time into the bin from distances that they would never have believed possible. It goes without saying that you need know nothing yourself about the techniques of ball-throwing.

Agenda: the client's, not the coach's

Coaching is unlike many other kinds of one-to-one relationship in that the coach has no agenda of his or her own. For instance, a doctor may have a favourite and useful drug that they diagnose for tonsillitis. A teacher may have a curriculum which the pupil must follow, even if both teacher and pupil are uninterested in the topics. A therapist may feel they have to follow the philosophy of the particular 'school' of psychotherapy that trained them – and so on.

Coaching starts and finishes with the client's agenda. This is because coaching is about change. In one episode of the BBC comedy series, *Rab C. Nesbitt*, the appallingly scruffy hero and epitome of unhealthy living goes to the doctor complaining about a stomach-ache and a cough. The doctor tells him to eat a proper diet and to give up smoking. Rab's immortal reply is 'I didna' come here to change my diet or give up smoking, I came to get cured!' If the client does not want to change, there cannot be any coaching.

Clients come to coaching because they want to change their lives and get results which show that change has happened. This may be about improving relationships, changing jobs or acquiring new skills.

The coach's role

So what is it appropriate for the coach to do? This is what I believe it comes down to:

- To ask the questions which establish the client's agenda.
- To hold onto this as the *only* agenda for the coaching.
- To ask the questions which uncover the blocks and fears which are preventing them reaching their goals.
- To hold onto the agenda for and with the client when things get rough, for instance when negative inner voices begin to sabotage the progress that the client is making.
- To remain unattached to whether or not the client achieves their goals while also eagerly wanting the client to do well. 'Attachment' could mean that the coach cares more about being a 'clever' coach than truly helping the client.
- To help the client take action.
- To identify what learning has happened during the whole process.

It is not the coach's role to provide answers, to try to do the learning for the client or to pose as the client's superior in any way.

The three levels of listening

Authentic listening is the most fundamental coaching skill of all. Real listening is very hard work, so perhaps it's not surprising

Table 10.1 Communicating non-acceptance

Comment	Effect conveyed to the other person
I'm sure you needn't worry about that.	Trivializes the other person's worry.
Time will heal – you'll come to terms with it eventually.	You have resorted to cliché because you can't be bothered to think of anything else to say.
Other people cope with far worse things – buck up!	Diminishes the other person.
Don't you think you should . . . ?	Preaching – implies that you know best.
Can we move on here to the really important issues?	Impatience – your concerns are more important.
I think you're right, the real problem is with someone else.	Colluding – covers up the problem.

that it is very rare to have the experience of being listened to with total attention. Many of us pride ourselves on being 'good listeners'. To admit to being a bad listener is rare.

Listening is about communicating acceptance. When we don't listen properly, we communicate non-acceptance. Table 10.1 gives some examples.

Listening is the primary tool of a coach. To do it well you have to be 'fully present' for the client. This means:

- keeping your own stuff well out of the way – for instance, setting aside your own preoccupations with relationships, health, work;
- preparing for the client with a few moments of quiet before you meet;
- monitoring your own listening while the client is talking.

The US-based Coaches Training Institute helpfully identifies three levels of listening. (See their book, *Co-Active Coaching*, by Laura Whitworth *et al.*)

Level 1

This is the level the client is at. At this level you are thinking about yourself. You are concentrating on *What do I want? What do I feel? How do I express this?* As a client, this is fine – it is what the coach is asking you to do. For instance, if you go to your doctor, it is right that you describe your symptoms, or describe your emotional state. As a coach, you need to get beyond Level 1. If you stay at Level 1, you will start looking too closely at yourself. *Was that a good question? What on earth do I ask next? Wasn't that clever of me?* As soon as you find yourself thinking these types of thought, it is time to re-concentrate on the client.

Level 1 listening is not effective for coaching. Symptoms of Level 1 listening are when you find yourself:

- giving advice;
- talking about your own experiences;
- feeling irritated with the client;
- nagging;
- addressing your own agenda instead of the client's.

Level 2

At this level, you are concentrating hard on the client. Your curiosity is aroused about this client. You are hearing his or her values expressed in what they say. You are allying yourself with him or her, concentrating without judgement on what he or she is trying to say. You and the client are locked in a joint bubble of concern. There is enormous empathy, concern, shared intuition and creativity. You are holding the client's agenda successfully. You are observing the client closely and your body language is probably naturally mirroring what the client is doing and saying.

The conversation flows seamlessly because the coach is so attuned to the client. At this level, you will be able to paraphrase and summarize exactly what the client has been trying to tell you and you are beginning to get some insights into what life would be like if you were inside this client's head. Your questions are highly focused. As a coach, you must be able to do Level 2 listening and most coaching will take place at this level.

Level 3

At Level 3 you are super-aware. This level has been called 'global listening' or 'radio field listening'. You are able to identify with the client and you are listening hard. But you are also aware of everything else that is going on. Not only are you aware of everything else that is going on in the room – the quiet tick of the clock, the subdued noise of laughter from neighbouring rooms – but also the nuances.

Here you see yourself and the client engaged in the dance that is any coach–client conversation. You are hearing the underlying music – what is *not* being said overtly but is being *implied*. You are aware of tiny changes in the client's posture, and your own. You are aware of when the client's voice has dropped or when there is a fleeting change of colour in his or her face. You are alert to subtle changes in the energy level between you.

At this level your intuition is fully switched on and is operating well – you trust it. You are prepared to follow your instinct that you and the client are on the right or wrong track. You are able to take risks confidently and draw the client's attention to what is happening in the here and now.

A format for a coaching session

Let's imagine that you are going to do some coaching. This may be a five-minute one-to-one as part of a general session of teaching, or it may be the full-blown two-hour sessions that I now typically have with executive clients. This is a format that I find useful. Adapt it to suit your own situation and purposes.

Catching up on last time

Where you and the client have agreed 'homework' between sessions, it is vital to find out what has happened. Useful questions to ask here are:

- What's happened since we last met?
- How did you get on with the work we agreed you would do?
- What have you learnt?

The last is a particularly useful question. Often clients have not done their homework for all sorts of good or apparently silly reasons. There will be learning in it, whatever has happened.

Goals for this session

Coaching is about change. If there is no will to change then there can't be any coaching. It is useful to pinpoint specific goals for the coaching. Useful questions here are:

- What would you like to have achieved, specifically, by the time we finish this session?
- What would achieving that goal do for you?
- Of those goals, what's their order of priority for you?

Looking at the facts

The point of this phase is for the client, not you, to understand what the known facts of the situation are. This is what the writer Edward de Bono calls 'White Hat' thinking in his book *Six Thinking Hats*. White Hat thinking is about facts, reality and certainty. It often gets muddled up with 'Red Hat' thinking – excitement, prejudice, fear and other kinds of attachment to ideas for emotional reasons. Red Hat thinking is also valuable because feelings are important, but it is helpful to separate them out. Useful questions here are:

- What's preventing the ideal from happening?
- Who's involved here?

- What are the facts?
- Who owns this problem?

Generating options

Brainstorming can be a useful skill here, especially for clients who seem stuck or helpless or when there are so many possibilities that it is difficult to choose between them. Introduce it by asking permission and explaining the 'rules' – many clients think they know what brainstorming is but show that they don't by mentioning an idea and then immediately evaluating it. The essence of brainstorming is that any idea, however silly, is encouraged at the first stage.

Brainstorming Stage 1
- Any idea however ridiculous or outrageous is permitted.
- All ideas are jotted down (agree which one of you will do this).
- No evaluation of ideas is permitted at the first stage – e.g. no raised eyebrows, indrawn breath and so on.

This stage goes on until all ideas are exhausted.

Brainstorming Stage 2
Agree the criteria for evaluating the ideas – e.g. how will you judge whether any of these ideas are useful or not? Look for several criteria – e.g. cost, practicality, speed and so on.

Brainstorming Stage 3
The ideas are evaluated – by the client not by you.

Brainstorming Stage 4
The ideas are turned into action.
As a coach, your role is to offer as many funny, absurd, sensible and practical ideas along with your client. Don't swamp the client – it should be an even-handed process.

Example
Anne was a client with three teenage children. She had recently been made redundant and had decided to set up a consulting practice.

Anne: My problem is I don't know where I'll work. I keep going round and round in my head and I can't come to any conclusion.

Coach: Can I make a suggestion here?

Anne: Yes, fine!

Coach: Let's brainstorm it and see what comes up. (*Coach then briefly reminds Anne of the rules of brainstorming.*)

Coach and client then produce about 12 possibilities which include: cordoning off an area of Anne's large dining room; hiring a room in a business centre; borrowing a room from a friend; turning the smallest bedroom into an office; converting the garden shed.

Coach: What criteria will you use for deciding which of these is the most useful?

Anne: Oh that's easy. I've got to have somewhere I can leave my papers. I've got to have somewhere that's private – I don't want people, especially my kids – looking over my shoulder reading my emails. And I want to be in touch with people all day – I don't fancy working entirely on my own. Cost is a factor too. I can spend about £7000 from my redundancy package, but I don't want to go over that. And I don't want to be too committed to a big continuing expense in case it doesn't work out.

Coach: So shall we evaluate each of these against that list?

(*Further two minutes where this happens.*)

Anne: Well. It's easy isn't it? It's got to be converting the shed. It's big enough and I can sort of leave home, yet I'm still in touch with the family. I can lock the door and leave my papers there. Also it will mean the house appreciates in value – so even if my business doesn't work out we will have a home office in the garden, which a lot of people might find attractive. And it's easily within my cash limit.

Coach: So what do you need to do now?

Anne: Get myself some builder's estimates and get on with it!

Moving forward

Coaching is essentially about three questions: What? So what? and What next? The key to this skill is the 'So what' and 'What next?' part of the coaching process. Without this skill, a coaching session can seem rambling and unfocused – just a nice chat with a pleasantly non-judgemental person.

Throughout the coaching session, you need to keep up the pace so that 'What next?' is constantly in view. It is a matter of judgement and experience to decide when it is appropriate to move to this phase.

Victims

Some clients get stuck in victim mode. Victims can prevent themselves learning from coaching because they are looking for ways to change others rather than themselves. They may have a terror of taking responsibility for themselves or even a fear of success. Symptoms of victim thinking are sentences that begin:

If only they'd . . .
I wish he or she would . . .
If only other people would . . .
I can't do this because they won't let me . . .
I can't . . .

You can challenge this kind of thinking by replying with a question. Table 10.2 gives some examples.

The key questions
The key questions for moving the client forward are:

- What do you really want?
- What will happen if you do nothing? (Usually the answer is that doing nothing will ensure failure – precisely what the client usually wishes to avoid.)
- What's your responsibility for change here?
- So what do you need to do to make the change?
- Who do you need to involve?
- What will support you?
- What can you do here?

Table 10.2 Replying with questions

Client says	Coach replies
If only they'd change their way of thinking...	How can you change *your* way of thinking?
I wish he or she would...	How can you alter the way *you* respond to him or her?
If only other people would...	What choices do you have when other people don't do what you want?
I can't do this because they won't let me...	In what ways are you giving other people the power to make these choices for you?
I can't...	Do you really mean, 'I won't'?

- How, exactly, will you makes these changes?
- By when?

Another excellent question is:

- What do you need to do to make sure that you don't succeed here?

The unexpectedness and cheek of this question usually makes clients laugh, but there is also rich learning in it too.

Accountability

Accountability is about how the client will account during the coaching for changes that he or she has agreed to make. Accountability is a tricky concept. It can seem too much like teacher–pupil or boss–subordinate if it is done in the wrong way. It does not mean finger-wagging if the client fails to carry out their commitment.

Differences from ordinary usage
Accountability in coaching is very different from boss–subordinate or parent–child accountability:

- It does mean that you, the coach, *hold the client to account for what the client has said he or she wishes to do to make changes*. It is the *client's agenda* and the client's ideas of where they want to change that is at the core.
- The client designs the items for accountability, not the coach.
- The client also designs *how* they want to be held accountable.
- As a coach you have *no attachment* to whether the client has carried out their tasks/homework or not. You want them to grow but you have no stake in their doing things to please *you*.
- There is no place for value judgements or blame.
- Whatever has happened there will be learning in it.

The accountability part of the process usually happens at or near the end of the session. The coach asks the client:

So what are you going to do to make these changes happen?

In hearing the client's reply, you press for SMART criteria:

- Specific: what exactly is the goal? The more specific and the less vague, the better.
- Measurable: how will you measure your success?
- Achievable: is it realistic and possible?
- Resourced: have you got the time and the money or other resources to do it?
- Timed: by when will you have done it?

Many clients will be very familiar with the SMART acronym because it is used so frequently in setting objectives in performance management systems.

You will also find it useful to ask whether whatever the client is suggesting is consistent with his or her core values. Look for up to three objectives for each session, depending on the length of the session and the subject and make a note of these objectives, even if you make very few other notes.

It is normal for clients to explore how you will respond on accountability because many of them will have the idea that it is just like delivering a piece of homework, especially if they have not carried out what was agreed. Explore this in the initial session and also when the client falters. Ask, 'How would you like me to work with you here? Does it help if we keep strictly to what you have suggested or should I be gentle?' This way you put the responsibility right back where it belongs – with the client.

Coaching is an apparently simple skill that is very demanding to do in practice. It needs empathy, discipline, self-awareness, courage, focus and a high degree of questioning skill. When it works, people can learn at breathtaking speed and in a way that leaves them feeling good about themselves. Anything seems possible. Coaching seems to me like a core skill for anyone interested in seeing adults develop. As a profession it is growing at an astonishing rate and seems to have much to offer as a mainstream way of helping adults learn.

Chapter 11

▶ Evaluating learning

School education is now clotted with attempts to measure the progress of learning. One recent estimate suggested that by the time he or she leaves full-time education, the average child will have been subjected to no fewer than 76 different tests, with all the stress and misery that these events generate.

SATs (standard assessment tasks) and their like were probably an inevitable reaction to the vague claims of a let-it-all-hang-out-everything-is-creative approach of the 1960s and 1970s. Before that, the only measures of success in education were the notorious eleven-plus, largely abandoned after the mid-1960s, and public examinations at 16 and 18. Now, there are not only SATs but league tables comparing one school with another and tables that will compare success rates at GCSE and A level in one year with those in another, plus debate about whether these exams are getting easier.

Depending on where you teach adults, you may be feeling the backdraught from all of this, too. Certainly, in the work that I do, exclusively now with people in organizations, many of my company's clients are interested to know how we will evaluate success. They are spending a lot of money and they want reassurance that their investment is likely to be realized.

Why evaluate?

I don't believe you can be serious as a teacher of adults without being interested in this question. Even in my very early days as a tutor I wanted to know the answer to the question: *is it working?* At the simplest level, I took falling or rising numbers of attendees at voluntary classes to be a reflection of how well I was doing, and I was right to do so, even though there can be many reasons other than your own prowess for changes in attendance patterns.

At the same time, you do also have to take a reasonably relaxed view. Anxiously awaiting my first-ever batch of A-level students' results, I remember a cynical colleague telling me that if the pass rate was high then the college would credit the students, whereas if it was low then it was my fault. Alas, we can see the same churlish syndrome at work today. If exam pass rates go down, then it is the responsibility of the teachers. If pass rates continue to rise, then it must because the standard is declining.

In spite of the review-by-tabloid that oppresses education, there are sound reasons for evaluating:

- No learning is ever undertaken unless it is to change and improve something. If it is worth doing at all, then you or your sponsor will want to know that improvement is likely.
- All training costs money. This is true when it is the 'wooden pounds' that are involved when the training is done internally by an organization using its own staff and premises for its own staff. It is also true when both trainers and trainees are volunteers. I donate a small percentage of my time as a trainer designating it 'gift work' but I make it a principle to let the recipient organization or person know what the value of that gift is. There is an opportunity cost for me in doing free work and often an opportunity cost for the client, too.
- All teachers, trainers and tutors worth their salt want to know how they compare with others doing similar work. When I was working in colleges of further education, it was very clear to me that some of my colleagues were effective and some, dealing with the same students and in the same subject, were not so effective. I wanted to know why and how this difference happened. Similarly, when I ran a training department, we delivered many apparently identical courses for similar participants. But some courses got very high 'marks' and some

did not. Patterns soon emerged when we tracked the same courses over time. It was crystal clear that the differentiating factor was the tutor. If you are that tutor, unless you know where you stand, you can't improve.

A word of caution: anyone who is serious about their teaching or training will be evaluating all the time, for instance by:

- asking people informally how they are doing and what they are learning;
- asking people informally what they think and feel about the quality of the event;
- observing who is looking happy, unhappy, bored or tired and investigating what is going on through informal discussion. You do not need forms to do evaluation. It's a bit like finding out that you are speaking prose all the time.

The truth is that you are evaluating all the time when you are a conscientious tutor.

Useful terms

There are a number of different terms in this arena that it is useful to define:

- *Evaluation* means a system of judging the benefit of teaching or training to participants or to the sponsoring organization.
- *Validation* means judging whether the training met the objectives set for it, regardless of whether the participants liked or enjoyed the training.
- *Assessment* means judging whether the teaching or training meets a national or international standard – for instance, the baccalaureate, A level, NVQ.

Who does the evaluating?

This may seem a strange question, but it is an important one. There is no proof that I know of which will show that a so-called 'independent' evaluation is any 'better' than one carried out by the tutor or institution itself. What is true is that you will get a different result, depending on who carries the evaluation out. No evaluation of one human being by another can be 'objective'. The opinions, bias, assumptions and knowledge of the observer inevitably get in the way.

Also, I believe it is a basic scientific principle that you cannot measure anything without altering it. So, for instance, if you press a ruler against paper to measure a distance, you will have altered the surface of the paper, however minimally. If you count the number of blackbird nests in a field as part of an ecological study, you may disturb the birds and thus alter the number of chicks they rear successfully.

This principle is even more obviously true of evaluating human learning. The presence of an observer changes the process, putting both participants and tutors on their guard and thus altering their behaviour. Sometimes this can produce gross distortions. There are many accounts from schools of how an approaching Ofsted (Office for Standards in Education) inspection means that children and lessons are rehearsed, that teachers and children can have nervous breakdowns and that an air of anxious despair can hang over the whole school, particularly if it has already been designated as 'failing'.

A colleague and I ran a particular course over many years and suggested that one of our sponsors might like to evaluate it. We insisted that an independent third party should do the evaluating. However, our faith in the process was dented by a number of things that happened during the evaluation itself. First, our evaluator appeared only sporadically during the course, so she missed large chunks of key activity. She also told us that she had only just had a baby and so was feeling 'a bit dippy'. Then, instead of remaining outside various group discussions as an observer, to our amazement and horror, she actually joined in, excusing herself by saying 'This is a subject I'm really interested in!' Finally, the consultancy hired by our commissioning client was a competitor of ours. Our participants realized this and told us that their loyalty was to us. When the evaluator rang them several months later for further comments, several people told us that they had given guarded replies, for this reason. We might also have suspected that our evaluator had every reason to downplay our success, though to be fair her eventual report was enthusiastic. As a final twist to possibly mixed motives, we learnt that six months later her company was offering an event that looked remarkably like a mirror of ours!

However, there is certainly a case for someone other than the tutor asking the questions. When you as the tutor ask the questions, you may get vague, or softer answers, as people don't want to be horrible and may dress up their criticisms to avoid hurting you. Alternatively, if for some reason they have taken a violent dislike to you, their negative comments may be more extreme than is really justified by whatever offence they believe you have caused.

Also, you may find it difficult to hear the comments of participants, especially if they are not put tactfully. I worked some years ago with a distinguished consultant, a world leader in his field. He told me that he had no interest whatsoever in hearing what participants had to say about him or his events because he was his own harshest critic and always knew when he was on form and when he was not. I attended a course he ran and found him shamelessly open about this in what he said to us at the opening session. 'Don't bother to think that you can redesign this event,' he announced calmly to the assembled participants – also people in the consulting and training business. 'I've been running it for 12 years and I've already heard any comment you are likely to make.'

For all these reasons, think carefully about who does the evaluation and put the answers you get into a cautious perspective.

What do you evaluate against?

Preparation for evaluation starts with a careful analysis of objectives (see page 86). If you don't have objectives for learning, then you have no prospect of evaluating anything.

It also starts with an analysis of what your learners already know. If you have no baseline, then you can't evaluate. For most tutors, the evaluation process will apparently fail at this point. Most of us cannot sit our learners down and subject them to tests of their existing knowledge and attitudes. The process is too loose and informal. Probably, like most of us, you will have to do this impressionistically on the basis of what participants tell you about their existing knowledge or skill and on your own observation in any activities you set them at the outset.

It is useful to look at evaluation in four stages. These are usually described as Levels 1, 2, 3 and 4.

Level 1: enjoyment

Level 1 is about the event. This level looks at what is happening during and at the end of an event. You are looking at it in its own setting, not afterwards. This level is really about how the participants enjoyed it and found it useful. They are evaluating the *teaching*, not the *learning*. To a large extent, they are evaluating *you*. At Level 1, you are asking for opinions on areas such as:

- Did you enjoy it?
- Was it useful?
- What do you think you have learnt?
- What comments do you have on the tutor(s)?
- What do you think of the venue?
- How did you feel about the joining instructions?

These questions, and others like them, are the foundations of the so-called 'Happy Sheet', distributed to participants at the end of an event. The down-putting phrase *Happy Sheet* is important. It suggests:

- This information is of no importance.
- Participants' minds are on going home and they don't care.
- People will write anything just to get away.
- All their remarks will be skewed to the 'happy' – i.e. to the positive.

I don't agree with the generally dismissive view of end-of-course evaluations. They do give pricelessly useful information as long as you put it into context. For a start, if you are running the same learning event more than once, you can benchmark one event against another. If you are running the same event but with different tutors, you can do the same. Where you ask people to give a numerical score for an event, you can average the scores, turn them into a percentage 'satisfaction score' and track them over weeks or even years. I have found that they are remarkably sensitive ways to look at 'customer satisfaction'.

Giving people a 1–7 scale is a useful way to look at how they feel about the event. Using such a scale, questions you should consider including at Level 1 are:

- How far did this course meet your objectives?
- How far did the course content meet your needs?
- How do you rate the tutors?
- How do you rate the venue?
- How do you rate the admin?
- What overall satisfaction score would you give this event?

You might also like to consider some open-ended questions such as:

- Which sessions do you think might be added, lengthened or shortened? What are your reasons here?
- What could we or should we do to improve this event?

There are a number of other, more informal ways you can do Level 1 evaluation. One that I like is the 'Graffiti Wall'. Stick several pieces of flipchart paper together so that they join up along a wall. Draw a huge 'wall' with large 'bricks' and invite participants to write their comments in a 'brick' (as many per person as they like) in felt-tip pen.

Health warnings about Level 1
The evaluators at Level 1 are the participants. Like any of us, they will have their preconceptions, prejudices and concerns. They may rate you high or low on the basis of impression, not reality, whatever that is. You may be the 'wrong' age, gender, sexual orientation, profession, race, religion or nationality, and have the 'wrong' appearance or credentials. Several well-known

experiments have shown, for instance, that the same 'lecturer' (actually an actor) could be introduced to different groups of matched students in a variety of guises. The more gilded and impressive his apparent credentials, the more highly the students rated him, even though he gave the same performance each time.

It is perfectly possible to dislike an event, but also to learn from it. The most unsatisfying course I ever attended as a participant involved qualifying to administer a particular psychometric questionnaire. The trainer had been to California and had, as he thought, learnt there from a master. He had us lying on the floor, holding hands, visualizing, 'doing personal work' and 'group process'. I have no objection to these approaches, indeed I use some of them myself, but they need to be used in the right place and at the right time and also need to be carried out with flair and conviction. My view was that these methods were inappropriate for the subject and that the tutor was fumbling for the right tone. I was there to learn about the construction of the questionnaire, its aims and how to administer it. I did in fact learn some of this, in spite of the tutor and his course. I went away fuming with frustration, but I now use that questionnaire all the time.

You can also really enjoy an event but fail to learn from it. All experienced tutors will have encountered the participant who loves courses, goes on them all the time, gives them rave reviews, but appears not to have done much learning in spite of innumerable opportunities to do so during the events.

Level 2: personal learning

Level 2 is about learning. It happens during, at the end and sometimes immediately after the event. Essentially Level 2 moves from whether or not people have enjoyed the event (Level 1) to whether they believe they have learnt from it. The formal way to assess learning is to apply some kind of test of achievement. Can participants now do something they couldn't do before? In craft subjects this will be easy to judge. Can people sew a straight seam, or build a strong wall or make a non-collapsing cake? In areas where physical prowess in involved, again it will be relatively easy to see. Can participants do yoga positions that defeated them when they began? Can they run a mile in ten minutes when previously they were out of breath after 30 seconds?

Where your subject is more about attitudes than about skills, you will have to be more ingenious. Apart from the informal ways of assessing, there are, again, a number of written forms you can use. A useful one is the so-called 'tea bag' technique. The name comes from the way 'the flavour just floods out'. Give each person a piece of paper where they have to complete these phrases:

I've learnt . . .	I'm puzzled . . .
I've discovered . . .	I can develop . . .
I've understood . . .	I'm disappointed . . .

You can do this at the end of each day, or at the end of the course. Vengeful participants can still use this format to tell you some 'home truths' as they see them, but essentially the onus here is on the participant to identify their learning, not to pass judgement on the tutor.

Another excellent idea is to introduce a 'learning log' where people write a brief account of their learning for each day, with a carbon copy for the tutor. These journals are often remarkable documents, which amaze both their authors and the tutor. They chart a learning journey in a way that is difficult to trap by other means.

Health warnings about Level 2
Most evaluation at this level is impressionistic and probably has to be. It assumes, for instance, that participants will know how much they have learnt, whereas this may not be the case. People may have done some significant learning but may not realize it. They may claim to have learnt something when they haven't.

Unless you can actually observe performance and see how and in what ways it has changed, you will be working on impression only. Even when you can observe performance, observer bias will come into the frame. For instance, one of my colleagues specializes in training people in presentation skills. This is one of the areas of our work where it is possible to make dramatic improvements in a very short time. But who says what constitutes an 'improvement'? Most comment on 'improvement' amounts to phrases such as 'I thought your opening sentence was much punchier' or 'You strike me as a lot more confident'. In other words, such comments are subjective rather than objective because they are going through the sieve of the observer's brain.

Level 3: applied learning

At Level 3 you are looking at the longer term. Can people actually apply what they have learnt to the 'real world'? Does their knowledge and skill stay with them after the course is over?

At Level 3 you are acknowledging that knowledge and skill has a half-life, or even a quarter-life. It decays unless it is reinforced and many things can get in the way of reinforcement. For instance, in my field, coaching and leadership development, the most obvious way in which knowledge and skill are destroyed is that the organization is indifferent to or actively hostile to what people have learnt on a course. A recently-returned course member may be trying really hard to apply and use their new-found skill, only to be greeted with phrases like, 'Oh she's been on a course. Never mind. She'll soon get over it.'

Less obviously, other interests and commitments press their claims. People may lack access to equipment and situations where they can use what they have learnt. For instance, if you go on a computer course, but lack a computer to practise on, you will soon find that you have forgotten most of what you learnt.

One way to track Level 3 learning is to return to participants six months or so after the event and ask them questions such as:

- What stays with you about the course?
- What are you doing differently as a result of what you learnt?
- What is the impact of what you are doing differently on you/ your colleagues/family?

There are a number of ways in which you can ask these questions. Choose from questionnaires, individual interviews and focus groups. All have their pluses and minuses.

Level 4: long-term impact

At this level, you are looking for the longest-term impact – on people's lives, and in work settings on the organization. This kind of evaluation is rarely attempted because it is difficult if not impossible to disentangle the effects of learning from many other factors.

An example from our own practice is a major project we did for a public sector client. The focus of the intervention was customer care. The need was acute: the organization was losing its customers and a survey showed the abysmally low opinion held about them by the majority of customers. The organization was also rapidly losing its customers to external competitors. So we had some valid pre-intervention data. We ran innumerable workshops and trained more than 3500 staff. At these workshops we administered Level 1 evaluations and were able to track the satisfaction of participants with the training they had received: mostly it was high or very high. After a year, a new customer survey was carried out by the same agency that had administered the first one. This showed that customer satisfaction had risen significantly. It also showed that the decline in business had been halted.

Naturally we were pleased with this data. However, we also had to accept that many factors other than our training were at play here. For instance, there was a major internal reorganization, a new managing director had been appointed, market conditions had changed, and so on. Also it was possible that the units attracted to the training were better run, so might have improved anyway. We still believe that our training was a significant factor in enhanced organizational performance, but it would be hard to prove conclusively that this was so.

Remember, also, that as at Level 1 people can dislike the intervention but still learn from it. An example was a series of workshops run in one organization with the aim of breaking through widespread complacency about its market position. It was mandatory to attend. Non-compliance was a way of life in this organization, and many staff found reasons to wriggle out of going. Those who did go described the day as 'brainwashing', and told colleagues who had not yet attended that the only good thing about the day was the lunch. However, it was remarkable that very soon afterwards, opinion in the organization about its financial position and about competitors was notably better informed and a number of business units began talking about doing 'competitor analysis' and 'strategic alliances' with other businesses. How far this could be attributed to the workshops and how far to other elements remains open to question. However, the department that ran the workshops has no doubt that it was an important trigger to greater realism, followed by action and change for the better.

Precision in evaluation

There is little precision possible in evaluating learning. If you think about the different levels, there is a steep decline in reliability and validity as you progress from Level 1 to Level 4. Unfortunately, this is precisely the opposite of the importance of the learning to individuals or to an organization. Organizations and governments invest in learning because they want long-term impact, but the further away you get from the learning event, the harder it is to say for certain that the learning was the cause of change.

You can try to put precision into evaluation, and just because it is difficult does not mean we should not try. However, remember:

- Much wasted effort can be spent on trying to measure and evaluate. Always ask if the effort spent on evaluation is justified by the quality of the information obtained.
- People can dislike an event (Level 1) but still learn from it.
- People can enjoy an event but fail to learn from it.

- There is always a tendency to measure the things that can be measured. These may not always be the most important. For instance, you cannot measure the pleasure of achievement, the delight in acquiring knowledge for its own sake, or the satisfaction of solving a long-standing problem. Yet these may be as important to individuals as anything to do with passing a test.
- Sometimes the most important things are intangible and cannot be measured. An example is a conversation I had recently with someone who had been on an event run some years back by a colleague and I. 'I don't remember anything else about the course,' said this person, 'except a blinding revelation: that *I was responsible for me.* This meant I couldn't be a victim, couldn't blame anyone, was responsible for my own moods and actions and couldn't be *made* to do anything. That piece of learning has literally changed my life.' I barely remembered the person or the event, but I recognized the passion and sincerity of these comments.

Much teaching and training comes down to acts of faith. We offer them and undertake them in the belief that they will be beneficial. There is also the argument that training, especially in organizations, is no longer an option, it is an investment. Employees see it as a right and as a privilege. The more people are on the fast track, the bigger the sum they expect to have spent on their development. The most successful organizations in the UK generally spend about 3 per cent of their payroll costs on training. If you fail to make the investment there could be a high price to pay. Aha! say the cynics. You cannot say that organizations are successful because of their training activity – perhaps these are successful organizations anyway. They have spare pre-tax money to spend, so they put it into training.

I personally believe this to be nonsense. At its best, learning is about flexibility. It is about learning how to learn. It is about problem solving. It is about growth. People and organizations that invest in this process are bound to benefit. But I can't prove it.

In the end there are no unequivocal answers to these challenges. Learning is about change and change in human beings is hard to track. A small change may have a huge effect and apparently big changes have little effect. As people charged with shaping learning, we have to hope that we are producing the biggest change with the least possible cost and effort and that time will show that we made a significant difference.

▶ Notes

Chapter 1

1 Postman, N. and Weingartner, C. (1969) *Teaching as a Subversive Activity*. Harmondsworth: Penguin.
2 Belbin, E. and Belbin, M. (1972) *Problems in Adult Retraining*. London: Heinemann.

Chapter 2

1 Bartlett, F.C. (1947) The measurement of human skill. *British Medical Journal*, 1.

Chapter 3

1 Tuckman, B.W. and Jensen, M.A. (1977) Stages of small group development. *Group and Organizational Studies*, 2(4).
2 Zander, A. (1951) Student motives and teaching methods in four informal adult classes. *Adult Education USA*, 2.
3 Whithall, J. (1956) An objective measure of a teacher's classroom interactions. *Journal of Educational Research*, 47.
4 Hoggart, R. (1969) The role of the teacher, in J. Rogers (ed.) *Teaching on Equal Terms*. London: BBC Publications.

Chapter 8

1 Paterson, R.W.K. (1970) The concept of discussion. *Studies in Adult Education*, 2(1).
2 Paterson, R.W.K. (1970) The concept of discussion. *Studies in Adult Education*, 2(1).
3 Johnson Abercrombie, M.L. (1969) *The Anatomy of Judgement.* Harmondsworth: Penguin.

Chapter 9

1 Kirk, P. (1976) The loneliness of the long-distance tutor. *Teaching at a Distance*, 7.
2 Two Open University students, quoted in MacKenzie, K. (1976) Student reactions to tutor comments on the tutor-marked assignment. *Teaching at a Distance*, 5.

▶ Index

Page numbers in *italics* refer to figures and tables.

▶ Bibliography

Abercrombie, M.L. Johnson (1969) *The Anatomy of Judgement.* Harmondsworth: Penguin.

Bee, F. and Bee, R. (1998) *Facilitation Skills.* London: IPD.

Belbin, E. and Belbin, R.M. (1972) *Problems in Adult Retraining.* London: Heinemann.

Berne, E. (1964) *Games People Play.* New York: Grove Press.

Bion, W.R. (1961) *Experiences in Groups.* New York: Basic Books.

Bloom, B. (ed.) (1956) *Taxonomy of Educational Objectives – Book 1, The Cognitive Domain.* London: Longman.

Casey, D. (1993) *Managing Learning in Organisations.* Buckingham: Open University Press.

Crane, T.G. (1998) *The Heart of Coaching.* San Diego, CA: FTA Press.

Cunningham, I. (1999) *The Wisdom of Strategic Learning,* 2nd edn. Aldershot: Gower.

De Bono, E. (1990) *Six Thinking Hats.* Harmondsworth: Penguin.

Eisenstadt, M. and Vincent, T. (2000) *The Knowledge Web – Learning and collaborating on the Net.* London: Kogan Page.

Gallwey, W.T. (1986) *The Inner Game of Tennis.* London: Pan.

Goleman, D. (1995) *Emotional Intelligence.* New York: Bantam Books.

Hay, J. (1992) *Transactional Analysis for Trainers.* Maidenhead: McGraw-Hill.

Heron, J. (1989) *The Facilitator's Handbook.* London: Kogan Page.

Honey, P. and Mumford, A. (1992) *Manual of Learning Styles.* Maidenhead: Peter Honey Publications.

Klein, J. (1965) *Working with Groups,* 2nd edn. London: Hutchinson.

Knowles, M.S. (1978) *The Adult Learner: A Neglected Species.* Houston, TX: Gulf Publishing Co.

Richardson, E. (1967) *Group Study for Teachers.* London: Routledge a Kegan Paul.

Rogers, A. (1986) *Teaching Adults.* Milton Keynes: Open University Pr

Rogers, C. (1970) *Encounter Groups.* London: Allen Lane.

Rogers, J. (1999) *Facilitating Groups.* London: Management Futures.

Salmon, G. (2000) *E-Moderating: The Key to Teaching and Learning line.* London: Kogan Page.

Schon, D.A. (1983) *The Reflective Practitioner.* New York: Basic Book

Thorndike, E.C. (1928) *Adult Learning.* Basingstoke: Macmillan.

Tuckman, B.W. and Jensen, M.A. (1977) Stages of small group dev ment revisited, *Group and Organisational Studies,* 2(4).

Whitworth, L., House, H. and Sandahl, P. (1998) *Co-Active Coa* Palo Alto, CA: Davies Black.